ANTIQUE WICKER

From the Heywood-Wakefield Catalog

With Price Guide

Schiffer Publishing Ltd

77 Lower Valley Road, Atglen, PA 19310

CONTENTS

Copyright © 1994 by
Schiffer Publishing, Ltd.
Library of Congress Catalog Number: 94-65608

Printed in The United States of America
ISBN: 0-88740-618-1

We are interested in hearing from authors
with book ideas on related topics.

Published by Schiffer Publishing Ltd.
77 Lower Valley Road
Atglen, PA 19310
Please write for a free catalog.
This book may be purchased from the publisher.
Please include $2.95 postage.
Try your bookstore first.

HEYWOOD-WAKEFIELD

Established in 1826

REED
FIBRE
AND
WOOD
FURNITURE

1929

Heywood-Wakefield Lines

In addition to Reed, Fibre, and Wood Furniture, the HEYWOOD-WAKEFIELD COMPANY manufactures Doll Carriages, Baby Carriages, School Furniture, Railway Car Seats, Motor Bus Seats, Theatre Chairs, Chair Cane, Cane Webbing and Cocoa Mats and Matting. Our catalogues, any or all of which our Warehouses will furnish on application, are as follows:

Furniture Catalogue

The *Reed and Fibre Section* of this catalogue shows complete suites of chair, arm chair, rocker, settee, foot rest, table, chaise longue, etc., etc., sold either in suites or as individual pieces, in addition to which is offered a large choice of individual patterns; bassinets, cribs, infants' wardrobes, children's chairs and rockers, cabinet chairs and high chairs, desks and desk chairs, davenports, day beds, dining chairs, ferneries, hampers, invalid chairs, lamps and porch furniture.

The *Factory Direct Section* shows the suites and individual pieces made for direct factory shipment from the Gardner, Mass., Wakefield, Mass., and Chicago, Ill., factories.

The *Wood Furniture Section* shows bank and office chairs, bathroom chairs and stools, bedroom chairs, benches, bentwood chairs, breakfast room suites, cabinet chairs, café chairs, children's chairs, Colonial chairs, couches, dining chairs, folding and portable chairs, hat-trees, high chairs, invalid chairs, kindergarten chairs, lawn furniture, living-room furniture, occasional chairs, Mission suites, rockers, steamer chairs, steel chairs, stools, typewriter chairs, tables, Normandy and Renaissance suites and single pieces, upholstered suites, desk and dinerette suites.

Baby Carriage Catalogue

The entire line of coaches, carriages, strollers, sulkies, etc., produced by Heywood-Wakefield. The final pages illustrate our complete line of juvenile merchandise.

School Furniture Catalogue

Entire line of Pressed Steel School Furniture, including complete sets of desks, recitation seats, commercial desks, as well as class and study room chairs, assembly seats, etc.

Theatre Chair Catalogue

This book illustrates and describes a complete line of chairs for theatre and auditorium use.

Outdoor, Arena, and Amusement Park Seat Catalogue

Chairs for baseball, racing, and other outdoor parks;—other chairs for indoor arenas, semi-outdoor moving picture houses, auditoriums, etc.

Folding and Steamer Chair Catalogue

Chairs which can be folded and stored in a small space. Furnished singly or in sections up to four.

Folding Portable Chair Catalogue

Folding wood chairs furnished singly or in sets with or without arm rests, kneeling benches or tablet arms.

Doll Carriage Catalogue

Illustrations with prices on latest line of doll carriages.

Cocoa Mat and Matting Catalogue

Door Mats for residences and public buildings. Floor Matting for aisle runners in retail stores, residences, and other buildings.

Motor Bus, Steam and Electric Car Seat Leaflets

Illustrations and price lists of kind desired sent upon application.

Reed Product Samples

Samples and prices of cane webbing, chair cane and reed, furnished upon application.

Finishes for Reed and Fibre Furniture

WITH the issuance of this catalogue, a new grading of finishes has been established on Heywood-Wakefield reed and fibre furniture. All finishes are placed and priced in one of three classifications—A, B or C. The list of finishes given below indicates the type of finish obtainable under each classification.

A *Finishes*

BLACK GLOSS: An Enamel Finish.
*CAFÉ AU LAIT: An Enamel Finish.
DARK BROWN: A Brown Enamel Finish.
FALLOW: A Light Brown Enamel Finish.
*FAWN: An Enamel Finish.

FRENCH GREY: An Enamel Finish.
FRENCH WALNUT: Dark Brown Stain Finish.
*IVORY: An Enamel Finish.
*JADE GREEN: An Enamel Finish.
*ORANGE: An Enamel Finish.

WAVERLY: A Light Green Enamel Finish.

B *Finishes*

ALLUSEN BLUE DECORATED: Blue-green Bronze; Shaded Allusen Bronze, Decorated Red and Gold.
BLUE GOLD DECORATED: Dark Blue with Gold Overtone, Decorated in Light Red, Orange and Oriental Green.
CHARLOTTE: Fawn Enamel with Brown Shading.
*FAWN ENAMEL DECORATED: A Fawn Finish, Decorated in Orange and Black.
FROSTED BROWN: Brown Enamel with Silver Overtone.
GREEN GOLD DECORATED: Grass Green with Gold Overtone, Decorated in Light Red, Black and Orange.
HARVEST SHADE DECORATED: Yellow-Green Bronze; Shaded Red-Gold Bronze, Decorated in Green and Red.
HOME: Brown Enamel with Brown Mahogany Shading.
*JADE GREEN DECORATED: A Jade Green Finish, Decorated in Orange and Black.
LAVENDER GOLD DECORATED: Deep Lavender with Gold Overtone, Decorated in Light Red, Black and Dark Blue.
*PARCHMENT: Light Yellow Enamel with Brown Overtone.
*RED ENAMEL DECORATED: A Red Enamel Finish, Decorated in Black and Green.
ROSE GOLD DECORATED: Rose Overtone Gold, Decorated in Black and Light Green.
SILVER BLUE DECORATED: Silver Shaded Light Blue, Decorated in Plum and Green.
LA BREA: A Fawn Enamel with Brown Shading.

C *Finishes*

ALLEGRA DECORATED: Parchment with Light Green Shading, Decorated Black and Red.
CHINESE GREEN DECORATED: Green Enamel with Black Shading, Decorated in Red and Gold.
CHINESE ORANGE DECORATED: Orange Enamel, Black Shading, Decorated in Green and Gold.
DIXIE DECORATED: Light Blue Enamel with Gold Overtone, Purple Shading, Decorated Green and Red.
*GOTHAM: Deep Ivory Enamel, Shaded Orange over Green Decoration.
*HAZE DECORATED: Light Yellow Enamel, Lavender Overtone, Decorated in Lavender and Black.
LA BREA DECORATED: Fawn Enamel with Brown Shading, Decorated in Green and Orange.
MORNING GLORY DECORATED: Orchid Enamel with Purple Shading, Decorated in Blue, Yellow and Green.
NEWTON DECORATED: Light Grey Enamel with Black Shading, Decorated in Blue and Red.
PEARL BRONZE DECORATED: Light Blue Enamel, Copper Gold Overtone, Decorated in Red, Black, Blue and Yellow.
*SERENE DECORATED: Orange Enamel, Green Overtone, Decorated in Jade, Black and Blue.
TAMPA DECORATED: Coral Enamel, Blue Overtone, Decorated in Green and Gold.
TIA JUANA DECORATED: Gold Bronze with Brown Shading, Decorated in Red and Green.

These finishes are particularly adapted to Stick Reed Furniture.

Luxury

In this luxurious setting of stick reed pieces are shown davenport R 845-60, end table R 839 G (page 7) and lamp R 734 E (page 72). The group is shown in Haze, Decorated, a C type finish. The upholstery is an 8 grade "Art Moderne" cloth.

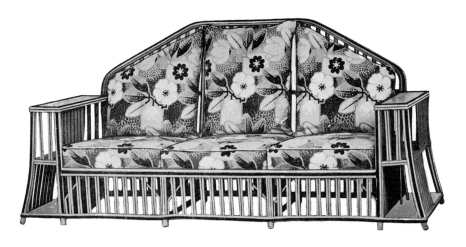

R 845 C   Reed Chair

Kapok Filled Pillow-Type Back Cushion and Spring Filled Seat Cushion. Width between Arms, 22 inches. Depth of Seat, 21 inches. Height of Back, 22 inches.

R 845-60   Reed Davenport

Kapok Filled Pillow-Type Back Cushion and Spring Filled Seat Cushion. Width between Arms, 60 inches. Depth of Seat, 24 inches. Height of Back, 24 inches.

R 845 CS   Reed Chair

Kapok Filled Pillow-Type Back Cushion and Spring Filled Seat Cushion. Width between Arms, 21½ inches. Depth of Seat, 22 inches. Height of Back, 24 inches.

R 843 G   Reed Table

A Moderne reed table which is good-looking and useful. The top measures 30 inches. It is 28 inches high.

R 844 G   Reed Table

An unusual "Art Moderne" reed table with wood shelves. The top measures 27 inches. It is 28 inches high.

R 839 G   Reed Table

An attractive and different reed end table. The top measures 24 x 12 inches. It is 22 inches high.

R 842 G   Reed Table

A handy, well made reed table of Moderne design. The top measures 28 x 14½ inches. It is 22 inches high.

For Finishes See Page 5

R 846 C   Reed Chair

Kapok Filled Pillow-Type Back Cushion and Spring Filled Seat Cushion. Width between Arms, 19½ inches. Depth of Seat, 24 inches. Height of Back, 21 inches.

R 846-60   Reed Davenport

Kapok Filled Pillow-Type Back Cushion and Spring Filled Seat Cushion. Width between Arms, 60 inches. Depth of Seat, 24 inches. Height of Back, 23 inches.

R 847 C   Reed Chair

Kapok Filled Pillow-Type Back Cushion and Spring Filled Seat Cushion. Width between Arms, 21½ inches. Depth of Seat, 26 inches. Height of Back, 23½ inches. This chair has a Book Pocket.

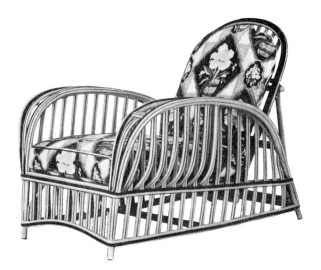

R 840 G   Reed Table

An extremely simple, yet attractive, reed end or coffee table. The top measures 21 x 14 inches. It is 22 inches high.

R 841 G   Reed Table

An end, console or wall reed table, designed in the Moderne manner. The top measures 30 x 13 inches. It is 22 inches high.

R 852   Reed Foot Rest

A Moderne reed foot rest with a comfortable, spring filled cushion. Top, 34 x 18 inches. Height to top of cushion, 15 inches.

R 853 C   Reed Chair

Kapok Filled Pillow-Type Back Cushion and Spring Filled Seat Cushion. Heavy type adjustable back. Width between Arms, 21½ inches. Depth of Seat, 26 inches. Height of Back, 25 inches. This chair has a Book Pocket.

For Finishes See Page 5

R 696 C   Reed Chair

Spring Filled Seat Cushion. Width between
Arms, 19 inches. Depth of Seat, 20 inches.
Height of Back, 17 inches.

R 696-48   Reed Settee

Spring Filled Seat Cushion. Width between Arms, 48 inches.
Depth of Seat, 22 inches. Height of Back, 17 inches.

R 696 D   Reed Rocker

Spring Filled Seat Cushion. Width between
Arms, 19 inches. Depth of Seat, 20 inches.
Height of Back, 17 inches.

R 696 CX   Reed Chair

Spring Filled Seat Cushion. Pad Back Cushion. Width between Arms, 19 inches. Depth
of Seat, 20 inches. Height of Back, 17
inches.

R 696-48 X   Reed Settee

Spring Filled Seat Cushion. Pad Back Cushion. Width between
Arms, 48 inches. Depth of Seat, 22 inches. Height of Back, 17
inches.

R 696 DX   Reed Rocker

Spring Filled Seat Cushion. Pad Back Cushion. Width between Arms, 19 inches. Depth
of Seat, 20 inches. Height of Back, 17
inches.

For Finishes See Page 5

Smartness

Chair R 847 C (page 8) in Serene, Decorated, a C type finish, is featured in this group which includes end table R 840 G (page 8) and lamp R 556 E (page 73). The "Art Moderne" cloth on the chair is an 8 grade upholstery. In its modernistic stick reed furniture Heywood-Wakefield has embodied unusual designs with extraordinary comfort.

R 727 CX   Reed Chair
Spring Filled Seat Cushion over Spring Construction. Pad Back. Width between Arms, 19½ inches. Depth of Seat, 19½ inches. Height of Back, 19 inches.

R 727-60 X   Reed Davenport
Spring Filled Seat Cushion over Spring Construction. Pad Back. Width between Arms, 60 inches. Depth of Seat, 24 inches. Height of Back, 21 inches.

R 727-60   Reed Davenport
This pattern is the same as the above, but the back is not upholstered,—similar to the chairs below. Width between Arms, 60 inches. Depth of Seat, 24 inches. Height of Back, 21 inches.

R 727 DX   Reed Rocker
Spring Filled Seat Cushion over Spring Construction. Pad Back. Width between Arms, 19½ inches. Depth of Seat, 19½ inches. Height of Back, 19 inches.

R 727 C   Reed Chair
Spring Filled Seat Cushion over Spring Construction. Width between Arms, 19½ inches. Depth of Seat, 19½ inches. Height of Back, 19 inches.

R 820 G   Reed Table
An octagonal designed reed table with beautifully turned wood legs. The top measures 28 inches. It is 30 inches high.

R 727 D   Reed Rocker
Spring Filled Seat Cushion over Spring Construction. Width between Arms, 19½ inches. Depth of Seat, 19½ inches. Height of Back, 19 inches.

For Finishes See Page 5

R 729-48   Reed Settee

Removable Spring Cushion. Width between Arms, 48 inches. Depth of Seat, 22 inches. Height of Back, 20 inches.

R 729 C   Reed Chair

Removable Spring Cushion. Width between Arms, 18½ inches. Depth of Seat, 19½ inches. Height of Back, 19 inches.

R 729 D   Reed Rocker

Removable Spring Cushion. Width between Arms, 18½ inches. Depth of Seat, 19½ inches. Height of Back, 19 inches.

R 729-48 X   Reed Settee

Removable Spring Cushion. Pad Back. Width between Arms, 48 inches. Depth of Seat, 22 inches. Height of Back, 20 inches.

This stick reed suite is woven of pre-colored reeds and is supplied only in Artone finish—an attractive combination of orange and brown reeds hand-woven over a light green frame. The upholstery illustrated is Troysco grade 5 with hand-blocked design. However, any of our regular upholsteries may be used on this set.

R 729 CX   Reed Chair

Removable Spring Cushion. Pad Back. Width between Arms, 18½ inches. Depth of Seat, 19½ inches. Height of Back, 19 inches.

R 729 DX   Reed Rocker

Removable Spring Cushion. Pad Back. Width between Arms, 18½ inches. Depth of Seat, 19½ inches. Height of Back, 19 inches.

For Finishes See Page 5

R 729 G   Reed Table

This reed table can be supplied only in the
Artone Finish described on Page 12. It is
hand-woven of pre-colored reeds. The top
measures 22 x 42 inches. It is 30 inches high.

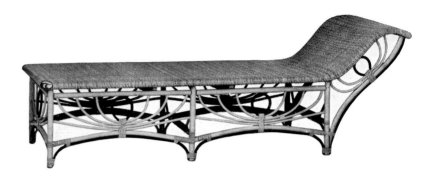

R 803   Reed Couch

The over-all length of this couch is 72 inches. The width over
all is 25 inches.

R 663 C   Reed Chair

Spring Filled Seat and Back Cushions.
Width between Arms, 21 inches. Depth of
Seat, 25 inches. Height of Back, 23 inches.

R 803 X   Reed Couch

Shown with pillow cushions. The over-all length of this couch is
72 inches. The width over all is 25 inches.

R 800 C   Reed Chair

Spring Filled Seat Cushion with Pillow
Back. Width between Arms, 21 inches.
Depth of Seat, 25 inches. Height of Back,
23 inches.

For Finishes See Page 5

Decorative appeal

These two pieces of the R 825 suite (page 47) suggest the decorative appeal of Heywood-Wakefield reed and fibre furniture. The chair and table are shown in Dixie, Decorated, an attractive C type finish. The upholstering used on the seat cushion is an attractive 3 grade cretonne. The R 825 is a new, reasonably priced suite that is sure to prove a big seller.

R 699 C   Reed Chair
Spring Filled Seat Cushion. Width between
Arms, 20 inches. Depth of Seat, 23 inches.
Height of Back, 22 inches.

R 699 CX   Reed Chair
Spring Filled Seat Cushion. Width between
Arms, 20 inches. Depth of Seat, 23 inches.
Height of Back, 22 inches.

R 698 CX   Reed Chair
Spring Filled Seat Cushion. Width between
Arms, 20½ inches. Depth of Seat, 21 inches.
Height of Back, 28 inches.

R 698 CXX   Reed Chair
Spring Filled Seat Cushion. Width between
Arms, 20½ inches. Depth of Seat, 21 inches.
Height of Back, 28 inches.

R 802   Reed Foot Rest
Pillow Cushion. This reed foot rest may be
used with the R 801 C chair. The top
measures 26 x 21½ inches. It is 13 inches
high.

This illustration shows the R 802 foot rest and the R 801 C chair
used together. This group makes a very comfortable combination.

R 801 C   Reed Chair
Spring Filled Seat Cushion. Width between
Arms, 21½ inches. Depth of Seat, 21 inches.
Height of Back, 31 inches.

For Finishes See Page 5

R 661 C   Reed Chair

Width between Arms, 20 inches. Depth of Seat, 18 inches. Height of Back, 24 inches.

R 661-48   Reed Settee

Width between Arms, 48 inches. Depth of Seat, 19 inches. Height of Back, 22 inches.

R 661 D   Reed Rocker

Width between Arms, 20 inches. Depth of Seat, 18 inches. Height of Back, 24 inches.

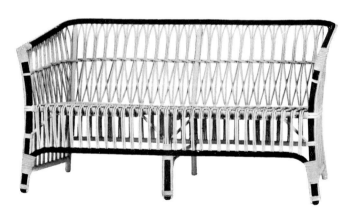

R 694 C   Reed Chair

Width between Arms, 18½ inches. Depth of Seat, 19 inches. Height of Back, 16 inches.

R 694-48   Reed Settee

Width between Arms, 48 inches. Depth of Seat, 20 inches. Height of Back, 16 inches.

R 694 D   Reed Rocker

Width between Arms, 18½ inches. Depth of Seat, 19 inches. Height of Back, 16 inches.

For Finishes See Page 5

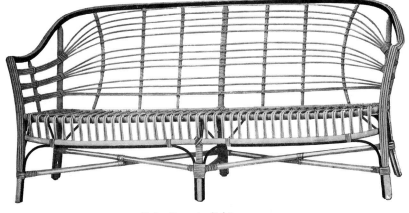

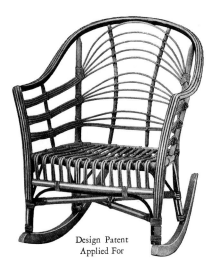

Design Patent Applied For

R 693-60   Reed Davenport

Width between Arms, 60 inches. Depth of Seat, 20 inches. Height of Back, 20 inches.

Design Patent
Applied For

R 693 C   Reed Chair

Width between Arms, 18½ inches. Depth of Seat, 18 inches. Height of Back, 20 inches.

R 693-36   Reed Settee

This pattern is the same as the above, but is shorter. Width between Arms, 36 inches. Depth of Seat, 18 inches. Height of Back, 20 inches.

Design Patent
Applied For

R 693 D   Reed Rocker

Width between Arms, 18½ inches. Depth of Seat, 18 inches. Height of Back, 20 inches.

R 695 C   Reed Chair

Width between Arms, 18½ inches. Depth of Seat, 18½ inches. Height of Back, 23 inches.

R 695-36   Reed Settee

Width between Arms, 36 inches. Depth of Seat, 18½ inches. Height of Back, 23 inches.

R 695 D   Reed Rocker

Width between Arms, 18½ inches. Depth of Seat, 18½ inches. Height of Back, 23 inches.

For Finishes See Page 5

This cheerful and comfortable stick reed group illustrates how the various pieces of the R 378 suite (shown on pages 20 and 21) may be upholstered. The pad back and seat cushions add little to the cost, but give the various pieces an unusually attractive appearance.

Cheerful and attractive

Heywood-Wakefield

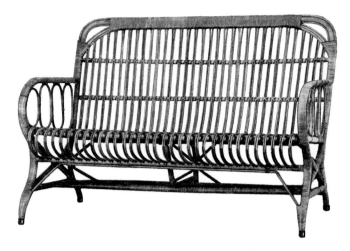

R 627 C Rattan Chair

Width between Arms, 19 inches. Depth of Seat, 17½ inches. Height of Back, 23 inches.

R 627-48 Rattan Settee

Width between Arms, 48 inches. Depth of Seat, 19 inches. Height of Back, 22 inches.

R 627 D Rattan Rocker

Width between Arms, 19 inches. Depth of Seat, 17½ inches. Height of Back, 29 inches.

R 627 A Rattan Chair

Width of Seat, 18 inches. Depth of Seat, 15 inches. Height of Back, 19 inches.

R 627 G Rattan Table

This table matches the suite shown on this page. It has a removable glass-bottom tray. The top measures 20 x 30 inches and it is 29 inches high.

R 690 G Reed Table

A reed table with a wood top and shelf. Top measures 34 x 18 inches. It is 30 inches high.

R 686 Reed Fernery

A reed fernery with a self-watering pan. Over-all dimensions, 36 x 11½ inches. Height, 30 inches.

For Finishes See Page 5

Heywood-Wakefield

R 378 A   Reed Chair

Width between Arms, 18½ inches. Depth of Seat, 18 inches. Height of Back, 22 inches.

R 378 AX   Reed Chair

Same as above, but upholstered as shown in group on Page 18.

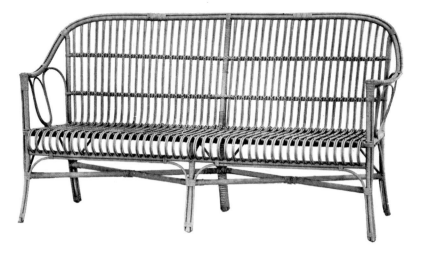

R 378-60   Reed Davenport

Width between Arms, 60 inches. Depth of Seat, 20 inches. Height of Back, 22 inches.

R 378-60 X   Reed Davenport

Same as above, but upholstered as shown in group on Page 18.

R 378 B   Reed Rocker

Width between Arms, 18½ inches. Depth of Seat, 18 inches. Height of Back, 24 inches.

R 378 BX   Reed Rocker

Same as above, but upholstered as shown in group on Page 18.

R 378 C   Reed Chair

Width between Arms, 19½ inches. Depth of Seat, 18 inches. Height of Back, 30 inches.

R 378 CX   Reed Chair

Same as above, but upholstered as shown in group on Page 18.

R 378-36   Reed Settee

Width between Arms, 36 inches. Depth of Seat, 19 inches. Height of Back, 22 inches.

R 378-36 X   Reed Settee

Same as above, but upholstered as shown in group on Page 18.

For Finishes See Page 5

R 378 D   Reed Rocker

Width between Arms, 19½ inches. Depth of Seat, 18 inches. Height of Back, 30 inches.

R 378 DX   Reed Rocker

Same as above, but upholstered as shown in Group on Page 18.

R 378 AS   Reed Chair

Width of Seat, 16 inches. Depth of Seat, 15 inches. Height of Back, 21 inches.

R 378 ASX   Reed Chair

Same as above, but upholstered as shown in group on Page 18.

R 378 J   Reed Chaise Longue

Width between Arms, 19½ inches. Length of Seat, 48 inches. Height of Back, 29 inches.

R 378 JX   Reed Chaise Longue

Same as above, but upholstered as shown in group on Page 18.

R 378 BS   Reed Rocker

Width of Seat, 16 inches. Depth of Seat, 15 inches. Height of Back, 23 inches.

R 378 BSX   Reed Rocker

Same as above, but upholstered as shown in group on Page 18.

R 378 G   Reed Table

This table matches the suite shown on this and the opposite page. The diameter of the wood top is 30 inches. Height of Table, 30 inches.

R 412   Reed Leg Rest

The leg rest used with the chairs shown on the opposite page. Length, 30 inches. Width, 20 inches.

R 691 GL   Reed Table

The wood top measures 34 x 20 inches. The table is 30 inches high.

R 691 GS   Reed Table

A smaller size of the table shown above. Top measures 30 x 15 inches. It is 30 inches high.

For Finishes See Page 5

Quality

Perhaps no chair in our reed and fibre line is
more expressive of Heywood-Wakefield
quality than the R 702 C (page 24) shown
here in Pearl Bronze Decorated, a beautiful C type finish. The spring-filled
seat cushion is upholstered in a
5 grade heavy craft cretonne.
The charming little end
or coffee table beside
the chair is R 702
GS (page 25).

R 721 C   Reed Chair

Spring Filled Seat Cushion over Spring Construction. Width between Arms, 19 inches. Depth of Seat, 19 inches. Height of Back, 23 inches.

R 721-60   Reed Davenport

Spring Filled Seat Cushion over Spring Construction. Width between Arms, 60 inches. Depth of Seat, 24 inches. Height of Back, 23 inches.

R 721 D   Reed Rocker

Spring Filled Seat Cushion over Spring Construction. Width between Arms, 19 inches. Depth of Seat, 19 inches. Height of Back, 23 inches.

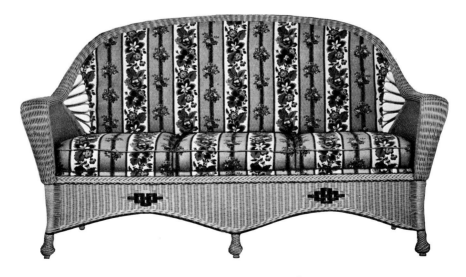

R 721 CX   Reed Chair

Spring Filled Seat Cushion over Spring Construction. Width between Arms, 19 inches. Depth of Seat, 19 inches. Height of Back, 23 inches.

R 721-60 X   Reed Davenport

Spring Filled Seat Cushion over Spring Construction. Width between Arms, 60 inches. Depth of Seat, 24 inches. Height of Back, 23 inches.

R 721 DX   Reed Rocker

Spring Filled Seat Cushion over Spring Construction. Width between Arms, 19 inches. Depth of Seat, 19 inches. Height of Back, 23 inches.

For Finishes See Page 5

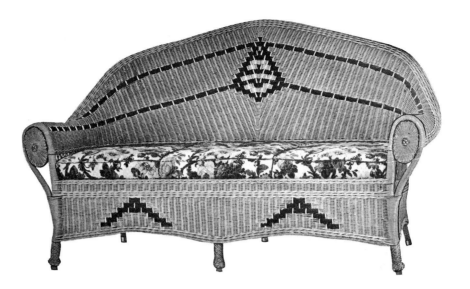

R 702 C   Reed Chair

Spring Filled Seat Cushion over Spring Construction. Width between Arms, 19 inches. Depth of Seat, 19½ inches. Height of Back, 24 inches.

R 702-60   Reed Davenport

Spring Filled Seat Cushion over Spring Construction. Width between Arms, 60 inches. Depth of Seat, 24 inches. Height of Back, 24 inches.

R 702 D   Reed Rocker

Spring Filled Seat Cushion over Spring Construction. Width between Arms, 19 inches. Depth of Seat, 19½ inches. Height of Back, 24 inches.

R 702 G   Reed Table

This table is designed to go with the R 702 Suite, but it may properly be used in almost any combination. Dimensions of Top, 20 x 48 inches. Height, 30 inches.

R 702 J   Reed Chaise Longue

Spring Filled Seat Cushion over Spring Construction. Width between Arms, 18 inches. Length of Seat, 48 inches. Height of Back, 24 inches.

R 702   Reed Fernery

A Fernery to match the R 702 Suite. Has self-watering pan. Height, 33 inches. Over-all measurements, 12 x 30 inches.

For Finishes See Page 5

R 557 Reed Foot Rest

Spring Filled Seat Cushion over Springs. Top, 20 x 27 inches. Height, 17 inches.

R 702 A   Reed Chair

The side chair of the suite shown on the opposite page. Width of Seat, 15¼ inches. Depth of Seat, 15 inches. Height of Back, 20½ inches.

R 702 W   Reed Desk

A graceful desk that is part of the suite shown on the opposite page. Top measures 22 x 38 inches. The desk is 29 inches high.

R 702 GS   Reed Table

A small table to match the suite on the opposite page. Dimensions of Top, 9½ x 20 inches. Height, 24 inches.

R 704 C   Reed Chair

Spring Filled Seat Cushion over Spring Construction. Width between Arms, 18 inches. Depth of Seat, 19 inches. Height of Back, 26 inches.

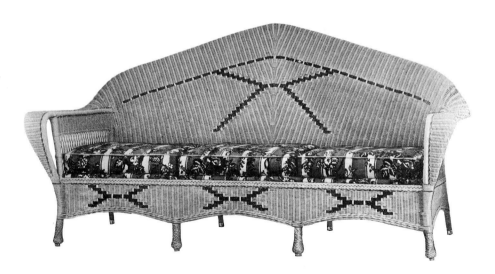

R 704-72   Reed Davenport

Spring Filled Seat Cushion over Spring Construction. Width between Arms, 72 inches. Depth of Seat, 24 inches. Height of Back, 25 inches.

R 704 D   Reed Rocker

Spring Filled Seat Cushion over Spring Construction. Width between Arms, 18 inches. Depth of Seat, 19 inches. Height of Back, 26 inches.

For Finishes See Page 5

R 436 C   Reed Chair

Spring Filled Seat Cushion over Spring Construction. Width between Arms, 19½ inches. Depth of Seat, 21 inches. Height of Back, 21½ inches.

R 436-60   Reed Davenport

Spring Filled Seat Cushion over Spring Construction. Width between Arms, 60 inches. Depth of Seat, 24 inches. Height of Back, 21½ inches. Shown with Pillows P 101.

R 436 D   Reed Rocker

Spring Filled Seat Cushion over Spring Construction. Width between Arms, 19½ inches. Depth of Seat, 21 inches. Height of Back, 21½ inches.

R 436 G   Reed Table

This table is part of the suite shown on this page. The top measures 25 x 40 inches. The table is 30 inches high.

R 375 E   Table Lamp

A well-designed table lamp woven of reed. Fitted for one electric light. The shade is 15 inches in diameter, and may be lined with cretonne or silk, as desired. The lamp is 24 inches high.

R 361 E   Floor Lamp

This lamp, woven of reed, is 69 inches high. It is fitted for two electric lights. The shade is lined with cretonne or silk as desired. Diameter of shade, 27 inches.

R 540   Reed Fernery

A reed fernery of striking design. It has a self-watering pan. Height, 32 inches. Over-all measurements, 10 x 30 inches.

For Finishes See Page 5

R 722 C   Reed Chair

Spring Filled Seat Cushion over Spring Construction. Width between Arms, 19 inches. Depth of Seat, 19½ inches. Height of Back, 22 inches.

R 722-60   Reed Davenport

Spring Filled Seat Cushion over Spring Construction. Width between Arms, 60 inches. Depth of Seat, 24 inches. Height of Back, 21½ inches.

R 722 D   Reed Rocker

Spring Filled Seat Cushion over Spring Construction. Width between Arms, 19 inches. Depth of Seat, 19½ inches. Height of Back, 22 inches.

R 722 CS   Reed Chair

Spring Filled Seat Cushion over Spring Construction. Width between Arms, 19 inches. Depth of Seat, 19½ inches. Height of Back, 28 inches.

R 722 J   Reed Chaise Longue

Spring Filled Seat Cushion over Spring Construction. Width between Arms, 20 inches. Length of Seat, 48 inches. Height of Back, 25 inches.

R 722 DS   Reed Rocker

Spring Filled Seat Cushion over Spring Construction. Width between Arms, 19 inches. Depth of Seat, 19½ inches. Height of Back, 28 inches.

For Finishes See Page 5

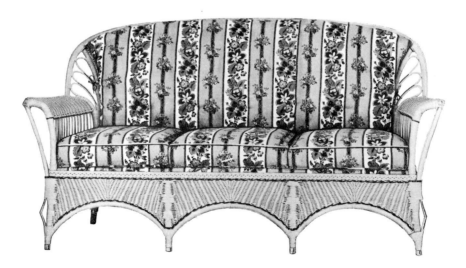

R 725 C   Reed Chair

Spring Filled Seat Cushion over Spring
Construction. Width between Arms, 18½
inches. Depth of Seat, 19½ inches. Height
of Back, 20 inches.

R 725-60   Reed Davenport

Spring Filled Seat Cushion over Spring Construction. Width between Arms, 60 inches. Depth of Seat, 24 inches. Height of Back,
26½ inches.

R 725 D   Reed Rocker

Spring Filled Seat Cushion over Spring Construction. Width between Arms, 18½
inches. Depth of Seat, 19½ inches. Height
of Back, 20 inches.

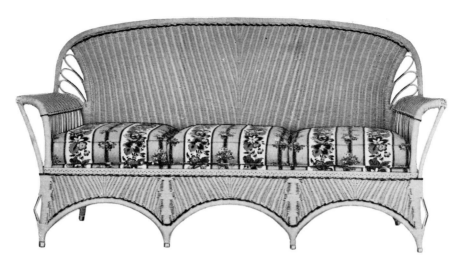

R 725 CX   Reed Chair

Spring Filled Seat Cushion over Spring
Construction. Pad Back. Width between
Arms, 18½ inches. Depth of Seat, 19½
inches. Height of Back, 20 inches.

R 725-60 X   Reed Davenport

Spring Filled Seat Cushion over Spring Construction. Pad Back.
Width between Arms, 60 inches. Depth of Seat, 24 inches. Height
of Back, 26½ inches.

R 725 DX   Reed Rocker

Spring Filled Seat Cushion over Spring
Construction. Pad Back. Width between
Arms, 18½ inches. Depth of Seat, 19½
inches. Height of Back, 20 inches.

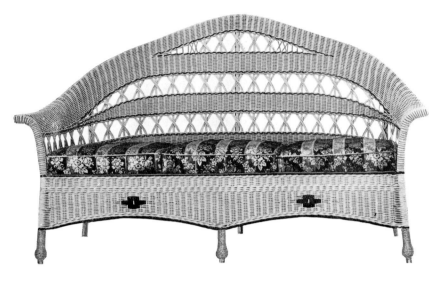

R 718 C   Reed Chair

Spring Filled Seat Cushion over Spring Construction. Width between Arms, 18 inches. Depth of Seat, 19½ inches. Height of Back, 25 inches.

R 718-60   Reed Davenport

Spring Filled Seat Cushion over Spring Construction. Width between Arms, 60 inches. Depth of Seat, 24 inches. Height of Back, 25 inches.

R 718 D   Reed Rocker

Spring Filled Seat Cushion over Spring Construction. Width between Arms, 18 inches. Depth of Seat, 19½ inches. Height of Back, 25 inches.

R 525-60   Reed Davenport

Spring Filled Seat Cushion over Spring Construction. Width between Arms, 60 inches. Depth of Seat, 24 inches. Height of Back, 22½ inches.

R 525 C   Reed Chair

Spring Filled Seat Cushion over Spring Construction. Width between Arms, 18½ inches. Depth of Seat, 19 inches. Height of Back, 22½ inches.

R 525 D   Reed Rocker

Spring Filled Seat Cushion over Spring Construction. Width between Arms, 18½ inches. Depth of Seat, 19 inches. Height of Back, 22½ inches.

For Finishes See Page 5

R 544 C Reed Chair

Spring Filled Seat Cushion over Spring Construction. Width between Arms, 19½ inches. Depth of Seat, 22 inches. Height of Back, 21 inches.

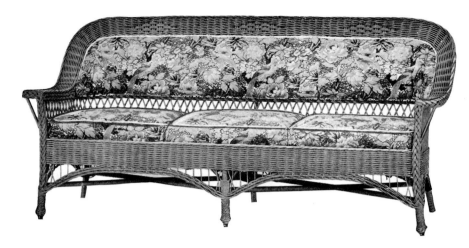

R 544-72 Reed Davenport

Spring Filled Seat Cushion over Spring Construction. Width between Arms, 72 inches. Depth of Seat, 24 inches. Height of Back, 21 inches.

R 544 D Reed Rocker

Spring Filled Seat Cushion over Spring Construction. Width between Arms, 19½ inches. Depth of Seat, 22 inches. Height of Back, 21 inches.

R 641 G Reed Table

The oval top measures 20 x 30 inches. Height of Table, 30 inches.

R 544-40 Reed Settee

Spring Filled Seat Cushion over Spring Construction. Width between Arms, 40 inches. Depth of Seat, 22 inches. Height of Back, 21 inches.

R 367 S Reed Fernery

An attractive fernery woven of reed. Has self-watering pan. It is 25 inches long, 11½ inches wide, 7 inches deep, and 30 inches high.

For Finishes See Page 5

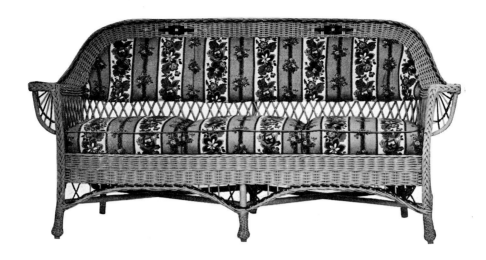

R 720 C Reed Chair

Removable Spring Cushion. Width between Arms, 18½ inches. Depth of Seat, 19½ inches. Height of Back, 20 inches.

R 720-60 Reed Davenport

Removable Spring Cushion. Width between Arms, 60 inches. Depth of Seat, 24 inches. Height of Back, 20 inches.

R 720 D Reed Rocker

Removable Spring Cushion. Width between Arms, 18½ inches. Depth of Seat, 19½ inches. Height of Back, 20 inches.

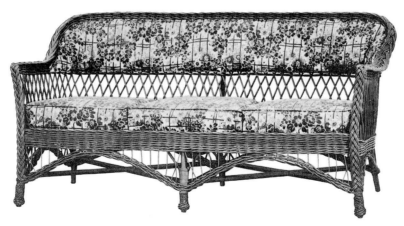

R 444 C Reed Chair

Removable Spring Cushion. Width between Arms, 18 inches. Depth of Seat, 19 inches. Height of Back, 16 inches.

R 444-60 Reed Davenport

Removable Spring Cushion. Width between Arms, 60 inches. Depth of Seat, 24 inches. Height of Back, 16 inches.

R 444-42 Reed Settee

This settee is the same pattern but shorter than the one illustrated above. It has a Removable Spring Cushion. Width between Arms, 42 inches. Depth of Seat, 22 inches. Height of Back, 16 inches.

R 444 D Reed Rocker

Removable Spring Cushion. Width between Arms, 18 inches. Depth of Seat, 19 inches. Height of Back, 16 inches.

For Finishes See Page 5

Reasonable in price

This davenport, R 653-60 (page 45), is from one
of the most popular suites ever introduced in
our line. The lamp is R 556 E (page 73).
The C type finish illustrated is La Brea,
Decorated, with 4 grade cretonne.
Another very attractive and
big-selling combination often ordered on this suite
is a plain-colored silk
mohair seat with
medallion tap-
estry back.

R 818 C Fibre Chair

Spring Filled Seat and Back Cushions over Spring Construction. Width between Arms, 19 inches. Depth of Seat, 18 inches. Height of Back, 24 inches.

R 818-60 Fibre Davenport

Spring Filled Seat and Back Cushions over Spring Construction. Width between Arms, 60 inches. Depth of Seat, 23 inches. Height of Back, 22 inches.

R 818 D Fibre Rocker

Spring Filled Seat and Back Cushions over Spring Construction. Width between Arms, 19 inches. Depth of Seat, 18 inches. Height of Back, 24 inches.

R 645 Fibre Fernery

Equipped with removable pan, 9 inches deep. Outside dimensions, 28 x 12 inches. Height, 30 inches.

R 821 A Fibre Chair

Width of Seat, 16 inches. Depth of Seat, 14 inches. Height of Back, 18 inches.

R 820 G Reed Table

An octagonal designed reed table with beautifully turned wood legs. The top measures 28 inches. It is 30 inches high.

For Finishes See Page 5

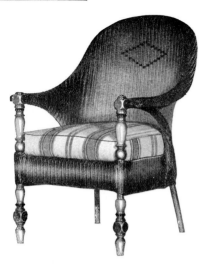

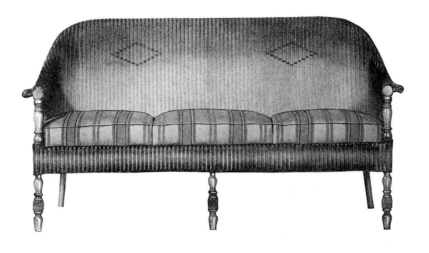

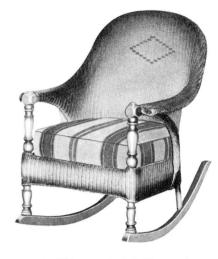

R 651 C   Period Fibre Chair

Spring Filled Seat Cushion over Spring Construction. Width between Arms, 19 inches. Depth of Seat, 19 inches. Height of Back, 21 inches.

R 651-60   Period Fibre Davenport

Spring Filled Seat Cushion over Spring Construction. Width between Arms, 60 inches. Depth of Seat, 24 inches. Height of Back, 19 inches.

R 651 D   Period Fibre Rocker

Spring Filled Seat Cushion over Spring Construction. Width between Arms, 19 inches. Depth of Seat, 19 inches. Height of Back, 21 inches.

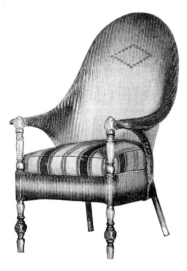

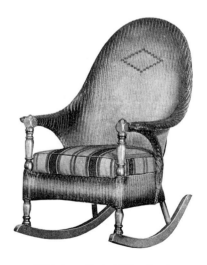

R 651 CS   Period Fibre Chair

Spring Filled Seat Cushion over Spring Construction. Width between Arms, 19 inches. Depth of Seat, 19 inches. Height of Back, 26 inches.

R 649 G   Period Fibre Table

An octagonal-top table to match the R 651 Suite. Top is 30 inches across. Height is 30 inches.

R 651 DS   Period Fibre Rocker

Spring Filled Seat Cushion over Spring Construction. Width between Arms, 19 inches. Depth of Seat, 19 inches. Height of Back, 26 inches.

For Finishes See Page 5

R 637 C   Fibre Chair

Spring Filled Seat Cushion over Spring Construction. Width between Arms, 19 inches. Depth of Seat, 21 inches. Height of Back, 14 inches.

R 637-60   Fibre Davenport

Spring Filled Seat Cushion over Spring Construction. Width between Arms, 60 inches. Depth of Seat, 24 inches. Height of Back, 14 inches.

R 637-42   Fibre Settee

This pattern is the same as the one above, but is shorter. It has Spring Filled Seat Cushion over Spring Construction. Width between Arms, 42 inches. Depth of Seat, 24 inches. Height of Back, 14 inches.

R 637 D   Fibre Rocker

Spring Filled Seat Cushion over Spring Construction. Width between Arms, 19 inches. Depth of Seat, 21 inches. Height of Back, 14 inches.

R 637   Fibre Fireside Seat

This curved seat has Spring Filled Seat Cushion over Springs. Top measures 39 x 18 inches. The seat is 18 inches high.

R 637 J   Fibre Chaise Longue

Spring Filled Seat Cushion over Spring Construction. Width between Arms, 22 inches. Length of Seat, 52 inches. Height of Back, 17 inches.

R 637 G   Fibre Table

This table may be used as davenport end table or console table. The top measures 25 x 12 inches. The table is 24½ inches high.

For Finishes See Page 5

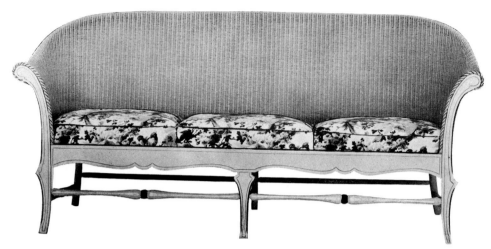

R 808 C   Fibre Chair

Spring Filled Seat Cushion over Springs. Width between Arms, 18 inches. Depth of Seat, 21 inches. Height of Back, 19 inches.

R 808-60   Fibre Davenport

Spring Filled Seat Cushion over Springs. Width between Arms, 60 inches. Depth of Seat, 22 inches. Height of Back, 19 inches.

R 808 D   Fibre Rocker

Spring Filled Seat Cushion over Springs. Width between Arms, 18 inches. Depth of Seat, 21 inches. Height of Back, 19 inches.

R 809   Fibre Foot Rest

This fibre foot rest matches the R 808 suite. Spring Seat. The top measures 22 x 16 inches. It is 17 inches high.

R 808 W   Fibre Desk

An attractive desk designed to be used with the R 808 suite. The top measures 28 x 18 inches. It is 30 inches high.

R 808 A   Fibre Chair

A small chair with a pillow cushion to be used with the R 808 W desk or as a side chair. Width between Arms, 17 inches. Depth of Seat, 18 inches. Height of Back, 19 inches.

For Finishes See Page 5

R 808 G   Fibre Table

An unusual wood and fibre table that has many uses. The top measures 36 x 24 inches. It is 30 inches high.

R 665 G   Fibre Table

An occasional or end table with a wood top which measures 24 x 12 inches. It is 24½ inches high.

R 672 G   Fibre Table

An occasional or end table with a book trough. The wood top measures 24 x 12 inches. It is 24½ inches high.

R 646   Fibre Fernery

Same as R 645, but shorter. Equipped with removable pan, 9 inches deep. Outside dimensions, 12 x 12 inches. Height, 30 inches.

R 689 G   Reed Table

A reed table of unique design with a wood top which measures 20 x 18 inches. It is 30 inches high.

R 9845 G   Fibre Table

A handsome table with wood top and fibre shelf. Top, 36 x 24 inches. Height, 30 inches.

R 645   Fibre Fernery

Equipped with removable pan, 9 inches deep. Outside dimensions, 28 x 12 inches. Height, 30 inches.

For Finishes See Page 5

Beauty

This group, consisting of Coxwell chair R 621 C
(page 39) and book trough table R 672 G
(page 66), typifies the craftsmanship and
beauty of Heywood-Wakefield furniture. The B type of finish illustrated
is La Brea. The spring-filled back
on the Coxwell chair is upholstered in a 10 grade
and the spring-filled
seat in a 9 grade
tapestry.

R 678 C   Fibre Chair

Spring Filled Seat Cushion over Spring Construction. Spring Filled Back. Width between Arms, 21 inches. Depth of Seat, 23 inches. Height of Back, 21 inches.

R 678-60   Fibre Davenport

Spring Filled Seat Cushion over Spring Construction. Spring Filled Back. Width between Arms, 60 inches. Depth of Seat, 23 inches. Height of Back, 21 inches.

R 621 C   Fibre Coxwell Chair

Spring Filled Seat Cushion over Spring Construction. Spring Filled Back. Width between Arms, 21 inches. Depth of Seat, 25 inches. Height of Back, 26 inches.

R 816 C   Fibre Chair

Spring Filled Seat Cushion over Spring Construction. Upholstered Arms. Spring Filled Back. Width between Arms, 19½ inches. Depth of Seat, 20 inches. Height of Back, 24 inches.

R 816-60   Fibre Davenport

Spring Filled Seat Cushion over Spring Construction. Upholstered Arms. Spring Filled Back. Width between Arms, 60 inches. Depth of Seat, 22 inches. Height of Back, 24 inches.

R 816 D   Fibre Rocker

Spring Filled Seat Cushion over Spring Construction. Upholstered Arms. Spring Filled Back. Width between Arms, 19½ inches. Depth of Seat, 20 inches. Height of Back 24 inches.

For Finishes See Page 5

R 491 C   Fibre Chair

Spring Filled Seat Cushion over Spring
Construction. Spring Filled Back. Width
between Arms, 20 inches. Depth of Seat,
20 inches. Height of Back, 20 inches.

R 491-72   Fibre Davenport

Spring Filled Seat Cushion over Spring Construction. Spring
Filled Back. Width between Arms, 72 inches. Depth of Seat, 24
inches. Height of Back, 20 inches.

R 491 D   Fibre Rocker

Spring Filled Seat Cushion over Spring
Construction. Spring Filled Back. Width
between Arms, 20 inches. Depth of Seat,
20 inches. Height of Back, 20 inches.

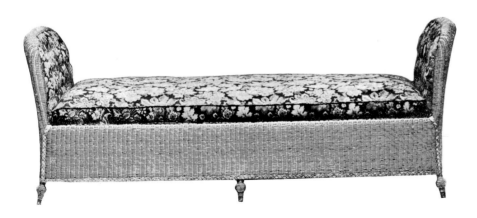

R 491 T   Fibre Day Bed

Spring Filled Seat Cushion over Spring Construction. This day
bed is 72 inches long and 28 inches wide.

R 491 J   Fibre Chaise Longue

Spring Filled Seat Cushion over Spring Construction. Spring
Filled Back. Width between Arms, 22 inches. Length of Seat, 50
inches. Height of Back, 26 inches.

For Finishes See Page 5

R 491 G　　　　Fibre Table

The table of the suite shown on the opposite page. The top measures 24 x 36 inches. The table is 30 inches high.

R 660 C　　　　Fibre Chair

Spring Filled Seat Cushion over Spring Construction. Width between Arms, 23 inches, Depth of Seat, 21 inches. Height of Back. 29 inches.

R 491 W　　　　Fibre Desk

A handsome fibre desk of graceful design. The top measures 36 x 24 inches. The desk is 30 inches in height.

R 658 C　　　　Fibre Chair

Spring Filled Seat Cushion over Spring Construction. Width between Arms, 20 inches. Depth of Seat, 20 inches. Height of Back, 15 inches.

R 658-60　　　　Fibre Davenport

Spring Filled Seat Cushion over Spring Construction. Width between Arms, 60 inches. Depth of Seat, 24 inches. Height of Back, 15 inches.

R 658 D　　　　Fibre Rocker

Spring Filled Seat Cushion over Spring Construction. Width between Arms, 20 inches. Depth of Seat, 20 inches. Height of Back, 15 inches.

For Finishes See Page 5

color harmony

Here are two popular, reasonably priced pieces
from our fibre furniture line, the R 636 C
(page 43) and the R 619 G (page 61).
Allegra, Decorated, a C type finish, is
illustrated on the chair and table.
This finish is bright, cheerful,
and blends in fine color har-
mony with the attrac-
tive 3 grade cretonne
used on the seat
cushion.

R 620 C   **Fibre Chair**

Spring Filled Seat Cushion over Spring
Construction. Width between Arms, 19
inches. Depth of Seat, 20 inches. Height of
Back, 23 inches.

R 620-60   **Fibre Davenport**

Spring Filled Seat Cushion over Spring Construction. Width between Arms, 60 inches. Depth of Seat, 24 inches. Height of
Back, 23 inches.

R 620 D   **Fibre Rocker**

Spring Filled Seat Cushion over Spring
Construction. Width between Arms, 19
inches. Depth of Seat, 20 inches. Height of
Back, 23 inches.

R 636 C   **Fibre Chair**

Spring Filled Seat Cushion over Spring
Construction. Width between Arms, 19
inches. Depth of Seat, 20 inches. Height of
Back, 23 inches.

R 636-60   **Fibre Davenport**

Spring Filled Seat Cushion over Spring Construction. Width
between Arms, 60 inches. Depth of Seat, 24 inches. Height of
Back, 23 inches.

R 636 D   **Fibre Rocker**

Spring Filled Seat Cushion over Spring
Construction. Width between Arms, 19
inches. Depth of Seat, 20 inches. Height of
Back, 23 inches.

For Finishes See Page 5

R 664 C Fibre Chair

Spring Filled Seat Cushion over Spring Construction. Width between Arms, 19 inches. Depth of Seat, 19½ inches. Height of Back, 21 inches.

R 664-60 Fibre Davenport

Spring Filled Seat Cushion over Spring Construction. Width between Arms, 60 inches. Depth of Seat, 24 inches. Height of Back, 21 inches.

R 664-72 Fibre Davenport

This pattern is the same as the above, but is longer. It has a Spring Filled Seat Cushion over Spring Construction Width between Arms, 72 inches. Depth of Seat, 24 inches. Height of Back, 21 inches.

R 664 D Fibre Rocker

Spring Filled Seat Cushion over Spring Construction. Width between Arms, 19 inches. Depth of Seat, 19½ inches. Height of Back, 21 inches.

R 664 CS Fibre Chair

Spring Filled Seat Cushion over Spring Construction. Width between Arms, 19 inches. Depth of Seat, 19½ inches. Height of Back, 27 inches.

R 664 J Fibre Chaise Longue

Spring Filled Seat Cushion over Spring Construction. Width between Arms, 21 inches. Length of Seat, 52 inches. Height of Back, 24 inches.

R 664 DS Fibre Rocker

Spring Filled Seat Cushion over Spring Construction. Width between Arms, 19 inches. Depth of Seat, 19½ inches. Height of Back, 27 inches.

For Finishes See Page 5

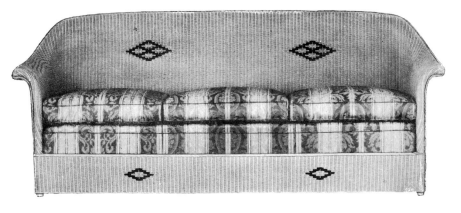

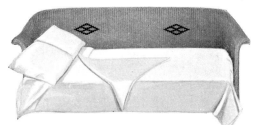

R 664   Fibre Davenport Bed

This davenport bed matches the suite shown on the opposite page. It has a Spring Filled Seat Cushion over Spring Construction. Width between Arms, 72 inches. Depth of Seat, 26 inches. Height of Back, 20 inches.

R 664   Fibre Davenport Bed

This view shows the davenport (illustrated at the left) made up as a bed. The size over all when open is 65 x 87 inches. The mattress size is 46 x 70 inches.

R 664 R   Fibre Reading Chair

Spring Filled Seat Cushion over Spring Construction. Width between Arms, 20 inches. Depth of Seat, 27 inches. Height of Back, 20 inches.

R 653 C   Fibre Chair

Spring Filled Seat Cushion over Spring Construction. Spring Filled Back. Width between Arms, 22 inches. Depth of Seat, 20 inches. Height of Back, 19 inches.

R 653-60   Fibre Davenport

Spring Filled Seat Cushion over Spring Construction. Spring Filled Back. Width between Arms, 60 inches. Depth of Seat, 24 inches. Height of Back, 19 inches.

R 653 D   Fibre Rocker

Spring Filled Seat Cushion over Spring Construction. Spring Filled Back. Width between Arms, 22 inches. Depth of Seat, 20 inches. Height of Back, 19 inches.

For Finishes See Page 5

R 835 C   Fibre Chair

Spring Filled Seat Cushion over Springs. Width between Arms, 19 inches. Depth of Seat, 20 inches. Height of Back, 26 inches.

R 835-60   Fibre Davenport

Spring Filled Seat Cushion over Springs. Width between Arms, 60 inches. Depth of Seat, 23 inches. Height of Back, 26 inches.

R 835 D   Fibre Rocker

Spring Filled Seat Cushion over Springs. Width between Arms, 19 inches. Depth of Seat, 20 inches. Height of Back, 26 inches.

R 838 G   Fibre Table

A generous sized table with an oval top which measures 38 x 22 inches. It is 30 inches high.

R 835 J   Fibre Chaise Longue

Spring Filled Seat Cushion over Springs. Width between Arms, 21 inches. Length of Seat, 52 inches. Height of Back, 26 inches.

R 9785   Fibre Fernery

A fernery woven of fibre. Has self-watering pan, 6 inches deep. Length over all, 31 inches. Width over all, 10 inches. Height, 31 inches.

For Finishes See Page 5

R 825 C   Fibre Chair

Spring Filled Seat Cushion over Springs. Width between Arms, 19 inches. Depth of Seat, 20 inches. Height of Back, 19 inches.

R 825-60   Fibre Davenport

Spring Filled Seat Cushion over Springs. Width between Arms, 60 inches. Depth of Seat, 23 inches. Height of Back, 19 inches.

R 825 D   Fibre Rocker

Spring Filled Seat Cushion over Springs. Width between Arms, 19 inches. Depth of Seat, 20 inches. Height of Back, 19 inches.

R 583 S   Fibre Fernery

An attractively woven fibre fernery with self-watering pan. This fernery is 24 inches long, 11 inches wide, 7 inches deep, and 30 inches high.

R 825 G   Fibre Table

A fibre table of good design with an attractively shaped top which measures 34 x 22 inches. It is 30 inches high.

R 9760   Fibre Foot Rest

Spring Filled Seat Cushion over Springs. Top, 23 x 20½ inches. Height, 18 inches.

For Finishes See Page 5

R 833 C   Fibre Chair

Spring Filled Seat Cushion over Springs.
Width between Arms, 19 inches. Depth of
Seat, 20 inches. Height of Back, 18 inches.

R 833-60   Fibre Davenport

Spring Filled Seat Cushion over Springs. Width between Arms,
60 inches. Depth of Seat, 23 inches. Height of Back, 18 inches.

R 833 D   Fibre Rocker

Spring Filled Seat Cushion over Springs.
Width between Arms, 19 inches. Depth of
Seat, 20 inches. Height of Back, 18 inches.

R 604 C   Fibre Chair

Spring Filled Seat Cushion over Spring
Construction. Width between Arms, 20
inches. Depth of Seat, 20 inches. Height of
Back, 19 inches.

R 604-60   Fibre Davenport

Spring Filled Seat Cushion over Spring Construction. Width
between Arms, 60 inches. Depth of Seat, 24 inches. Height of
Back, 19 inches.

R 604 D   Fibre Rocker

Spring Filled Seat Cushion over Spring
Construction. Width between Arms, 20
inches. Depth of Seat, 20 inches. Height of
Back, 19 inches.

For Finishes See Page 5

R 834 C   Fibre Chair

Spring Filled Seat Cushion over Springs.
Width between Arms, 19 inches. Depth of
Seat, 20 inches. Height of Back, 24 inches.

R 834-60   Fibre Davenport

Spring Filled Seat Cushion over Springs. Width between Arms,
60 inches. Depth of Seat, 23 inches. Height of Back, 24 inches.

R 834 D   Fibre Rocker

Spring Filled Seat Cushion over Springs.
Width between Arms, 19 inches. Depth of
Seat, 20 inches. Height of Back, 24 inches.

R 619 G   Fibre Table

An attractive table of new design with wood top
and shelf. The top measures 42 x 18 inches. The
table is 30 inches high.

R 834 J   Fibre Chaise Longue

Spring Filled Seat Cushion over Springs. Width between Arms,
21 inches. Length of Seat, 52 inches. Height of Back, 23 inches.

R 556 E   Floor Lamp

An attractive floor lamp woven
of fibre and fitted for two electric
lights. The shade is of fibre with
silk fringe. The diameter of the
shade is 22½ inches. The lamp
is 60 inches high.

For Finishes See Page 5

R 676 C   Fibre Chair

Spring Filled Seat Cushion over Spring
Construction. Width between Arms, 19
inches. Depth of Seat, 20 inches. Height of
Back, 20 inches.

R 676-60   Fibre Davenport

Spring Filled Seat Cushion over Spring Construction. Width
between Arms, 60 inches. Depth of Seat, 24 inches. Height of
Back, 20 inches.

R 676 D   Fibre Rocker

Spring Filled Seat Cushion over Spring
Construction. Width between Arms, 19
inches. Depth of Seat, 20 inches. Height of
Back, 20 inches.

R 677 C   Fibre Chair

Spring Filled Seat Cushion over Spring Construction. Width between Arms, 19 inches.
Depth of Seat, 20 inches. Height of Back,
27 inches.

R 675 G   Fibre Table

This table may be used with the suite shown
on this page. The top measures 32 x 16
inches. It is 30 inches high.

R 677 D   Fibre Rocker

Spring Filled Seat Cushion over Spring Construction. Width between Arms, 19 inches.
Depth of Seat, 20 inches. Height of Back,
27 inches.

For Finishes See Page 5

R 806 C   Fibre Chair

Spring Filled Seat Cushion over Springs.
Width between Arms, 19 inches. Depth of
Seat, 21 inches. Height of Back, 20 inches.

R 806-60   Fibre Davenport

Spring Filled Seat Cushion over Springs. Width between Arms,
60 inches. Depth of Seat, 24 inches. Height of Back, 20 inches.

R 806 D   Fibre Rocker

Spring Filled Seat Cushion over Springs.
Width between Arms, 19 inches. Depth of
Seat, 21 inches. Height of Back, 20 inches.

R 849 C   Fibre Chair

Width between Arms, 18½ inches. Depth
of Seat, 19 inches. Height of Back, 23½
inches.

R 849 CX   Fibre Chair

Same as above, but with Box Cushion over
Fibre Seat.

R 849-60   Fibre Davenport

Width between Arms, 60 inches. Depth of Seat, 22 inches.
Height of Back, 23½ inches.

R 849-60X   Fibre Davenport

Same as above, but with Box Cushion over Fibre Seat.

R 849 D   Fibre Rocker

Width between Arms, 18½ inches. Depth
of Seat, 19 inches. Height of Back, 23½
inches.

R 849 DX   Fibre Rocker

Same as above, but with Box Cushion over
Fibre Seat.

For Finishes See Page 5

R 609 C   Fibre Chair

Cane Seat. Width between Arms, 18 inches.
Depth of Seat, 19 inches. Height of Back,
21 inches.

R 609-44   Fibre Settee

Cane Seat. Width between Arms, 44 inches. Depth of Seat, 19
inches. Height of Back, 21 inches.

R 609 D   Fibre Rocker

Cane Seat. Width between Arms, 18 inches.
Depth of Seat, 19 inches. Height of Back,
21 inches.

R 609 CX   Fibre Chair

Box Cushion over Cane Seat. Width between Arms, 18 inches. Depth of Seat, 19
inches. Height of Back, 20 inches.

R 609-44 X   Fibre Settee

Box Cushion over Cane Seat. Width between Arms, 44 inches.
Depth of Seat, 19 inches. Height of Back, 20 inches.

R 609 DX   Fibre Rocker

Box Cushion over Cane Seat. Width between Arms, 18 inches. Depth of Seat, 19
inches. Height of Back, 20 inches.

For Finishes See Page 5

R 834 D   Fibre Rocker
Spring Filled Seat Cushion. Width between
Arms, 19 inches. Depth of Seat, 20 inches.
Height of Back, 24 inches.

R 835 D   Fibre Rocker
Spring Filled Seat Cushion. Width between
Arms, 19 inches. Depth of Seat, 20 inches.
Height of Back, 26 inches.

R 706 D   Reed Rocker
Removable Spring Cushion. Width between
Arms, 19 inches. Depth of Seat, 21½ inches.
Height of Back, 27 inches.

R 707 D   Reed Rocker
Removable Spring Cushion. Width between
Arms, 18 inches. Depth of Seat, 20 inches.
Height of Back, 25 inches.

R 660 C   Fibre Chair
Spring Filled Seat Cushion over Spring Construction. Width between Arms, 23 inches,
Depth of Seat, 21 inches. Height of Back,
29 inches.

R 719 D   Reed Rocker
Spring Filled Seat Cushion over Spring
Construction. Width between Arms, 19½
inches. Depth of Seat, 19½ inches. Height
of Back, 28 inches.

R 719 DX   Reed Rocker
Spring Filled Seat Cushion over Spring Construction. Pillow Top. Width between
Arms, 19½ inches. Depth of Seat, 19½
inches. Height of Back, 28 inches.

R 722 CS   Reed Chair
Spring Filled Seat Cushion over Spring
Construction. Width between Arms, 19
inches. Depth of Seat, 19½ inches. Height
of Back, 28 inches.

For Finishes See Page 5

R 637   Fibre Fireside Seat

This curved seat has Spring Filled Seat Cushion over Springs. Top measures 39 x 18 inches. The seat is 18 inches high.

R 804   Fibre Foot Rest

Woven Fibre Top. Top, 16 x 16 inches. Height, 15 inches.

R 804 X   Fibre Foot Rest

Same as above, but with removable pillow cushion.

R 809   Fibre Foot Rest

Spring Seat Construction. Top measures 22 x 16 inches. Height, 17 inches.

R 111   Reed Foot Rest

Box Cushion over Reed Seat. Top, 23 x 19 inches. Height, 15½ inches.

R 9760   Fibre Foot Rest

Spring Filled Seat Cushion over Springs. Top, 23 x 20½ inches. Height, 18 inches.

R 557   Reed Foot Rest

Spring Filled Seat Cushion over Springs. Top, 20 x 27 inches. Height, 17 inches.

R 659   Fibre Foot Rest

Spring Filled Seat Cushion over Spring Construction. Top 24 x 20½ inches. Height, 16 inches.

R 802   Reed Foot Rest

Made of reed with pillow cushion. Top, 26 x 21½ inches. Height, 13 inches.

For Finishes See Page 5

R 9706 T   Reed Day Bed

Spring Filled Seat Cushion over Spring Construction. Width, 26 inches. Length, 78 inches. Height, 29 inches. Shown with Bolster P 1.

R 823 T   Fibre Day Bed

Spring Filled Seat Cushion. Length, 72 inches. Width, 30 inches.

R 174   Reed Couch

With Woven Cane Top. The over-all length of this couch is 75 inches. The width over all is 25 inches.

R 76 J   Reed Chaise Longue

Box Cushion over Springs. Width between Arms, 21 inches. Length of Seat, 46 inches. Height of Back, 31 inches.

R 169   Reed Couch

Box Cushion over Springs. Length over all, 74 inches. Width of Couch, 28 inches.

For Finishes See Page 5

R 406 A   Reed Chair

Depth of Seat, 14½ inches. Height
of Back, 11½ inches. Height from
Floor, 17 inches.

R 702 A   Reed Chair

Width of Seat, 15¼ inches. Height of
Back, 20½ inches. Height from Floor, 18
inches.

R 821 A   Fibre Chair

Width of Seat, 16 inches. Depth
of Seat, 14 inches. Height of
Back, 18 inches.

R 561 A   Fibre Chair

Diameter of Seat, 15½ inches.
Height of Back, 21 inches.
Height from Floor, 18 inches.

R 808 A   Fibre Chair

Pillow Cushion. Width of Seat, 17 inches.
Height of Back, 19 inches. Depth of Seat,
18 inches.

R 9857 A
Reed and Fibre Chair

Width of Seat, 16 inches. Height
of Back, 18½ inches. Height
from floor, 18 inches.

R 1809 A   Reed Chair

Width of Seat, 18 inches. Height of
Back, 18½ inches. Height from
Floor, 17 inches.

R 192 A   Reed Chair

Width of Seat, 16½ inches. Height
of Back, 18 inches. Height from
Floor, 18 inches.

For Finishes See Page 5

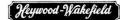

R 9168 A   Reed Chair

Width of Seat, 16 inches. Depth of Seat, 14 inches. Height of Back, 20 inches.

R 623 A   Reed Chair

Width of Seat, 16 inches. Depth of Seat, 14 inches. Height of Back, 17½ inches. Height from floor, 18 inches.

R 628 A   Fibre Chair

Width of Seat, 16 inches. Depth of Seat, 15 inches. Height of Back, 19 inches. Height from Floor, 18 inches.

R 697 A   Reed Chair

Width of Seat, 16 inches. Depth of Seat, 15 inches. Height of Back, 18½ inches. Height from floor, 18 inches.

R 413 A   Reed Chair

Depth of Seat, 13 inches. Height of Back, 12 inches. Height from Floor, 17½ inches.

R 518 A   Reed Chair

Width of Seat, 16 inches. Height of Back, 16 inches. Height from Floor, 18 inches.

R 432 A   Reed Chair

Width of Seat, 15 inches. Height of Back, 18 inches. Height from Floor, 18 inches.

R 656 A   Fibre Chair

Width of Seat, 16¼ inches. Depth of Seat, 14 inches. Height of Back, 18 inches.

For Finishes See Page 5

P 30   Pillow

A pillow of pleasing shape, lined with silk floss. This Pillow measures 24 x 24 inches. It is furnished in any desired upholstery, grades 3 to 10, inclusive.

P 101   Pillow

This attractively made pillow is 22 inches square. It is lined with silk floss, and may be covered with any desired upholstery, grades 3 to 10, inclusive.

P 19   Pillow

An attractive pillow that measures 21 x 21 inches. Lined with silk floss. Furnished to match the upholstery of any Heywood-Wakefield suite, grades 3 to 10, inclusive.

P 3   Pillow

This pillow is lined with silk floss. It is 21 inches long and 17 inches wide and may be secured to match the upholstery of any Heywood-Wakefield suite, grades 3 to 10, inclusive.

P 1   Bolster

This attractive bolster is 24 inches long and 7 inches deep. It is lined with silk floss and is furnished to match the upholstery of any Heywood-Wakefield suite, No. 3 grade to No. 10 grade, inclusive.

P 12   Pillow

This pillow of simple design may be covered with any desired upholstery in grades 3 to 10, inclusive. Lined with silk floss. This Pillow is 18 inches in diameter.

P 103   Pillow

A popular-shaped pillow, 18 inches in diameter. Lined with silk floss. It is furnished in upholstery to match any Heywood-Wakefield suite, grades 3 to 10, inclusive.

P 18   Pillow

This attractive shirred pillow is lined with silk floss. It is 18 inches in diameter. The Pillow is covered with upholstery to match any Heywood-Wakefield suite, grades 3 to 10, inclusive.

For Finishes See Page 5

R 668 G   **Fibre Table**

A good-looking table for use in living rooms, sun parlors, etc.
Top, 48 x 23 inches. Height, 30 inches.

R 702 G   **Reed Table**

A very attractive table which can be used in almost any combination. Top, 20 x 48 inches. Height, 30 inches.

R 436 G   **Reed Table**

A very attractive reed table for use in libraries,
living rooms, sun parlors, etc. Top, 40 x 25 inches
Height, 30 inches.

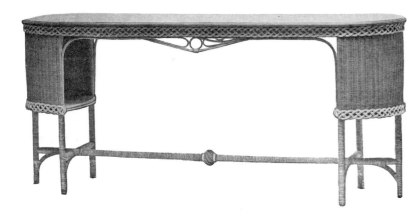

R 589 GL   **Fibre Table**

For use in libraries, living rooms, with davenports, etc. Top,
70 x 18½ inches. Height from Floor, 30 inches.

R 589 GS   **Fibre Table**

The smaller size of the table shown at the left. Top, 54 x 18½
inches. Height from Floor, 30 inches.

For Finishes See Page 5

R 491 G Fibre Table

For use in libraries, living rooms, etc. Has attractively shaped lower shelf. Top, 36 x 24 inches. Height, 30 inches.

R 540 G Reed Table

A table of unique shape which will look well in almost any combination. The wood top measures 19 x 48 inches. The height is 30 inches.

R 448 G Reed Table

A table which looks well in almost any room. Has two baskets, one at each end, and shelf. Top, 30 x 22 inches. Height, 30 inches.

R 839 G Reed Table

An attractive and different reed end table. The top measures 24 x 12 inches. It is 22 inches high.

R 844 G Reed Table

An unusual "Art Moderne" reed table with wood shelves. The top measures 27 inches. It is 28 inches high.

R 843 G Reed Table

A Moderne reed table which is good-looking and useful. The top measures 30 inches. It is 28 inches high.

R 820 G Reed Table

An octagonal designed reed table with beautifully turned wood legs. The top measures 28 inches. It is 30 inches high.

For Finishes See Page 5

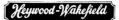

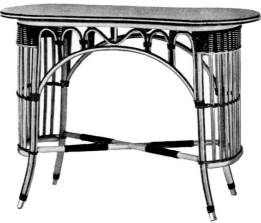

R 838 G　　　　Fibre Table

A generous sized table with an oval top which measures 38 x 22 inches. It is 30 inches high.

R 729 G　　　　Reed Table

This reed table can be supplied only in the Artone Finish described on Page 12. It is hand-woven of pre-colored reeds. The top measures 22 x 42 inches. It is 30 inches high.

R 403 G　　　　Reed Table

A reed table often used in libraries, living-rooms, with davenports, etc. Top measures 36 x 24 inches. Height, 30 inches.

R 681 G　　　　Reed Table

A console table for use in halls, reception or bed rooms. The top measures 36 x 16 inches. It is 30 inches high.

R 619 G　　　　Fibre Table

An attractive table of new design with wood top and shelf. The top measures 42 x 18 inches. The table is 30 inches high.

R 667 G　　　　Fibre Table

An attractive table with a wood top. The measurements of the top are 42 x 20 inches. It is 30 inches high.

For Finishes See Page 5

R 9845 G   Fibre Table

A handsome table with wood top and fibre shelf. Top, 36 x 24 inches. Height, 30 inches.

R 601 G   Fibre Table

A distinctively woven table with wood top for library and living room use. Top measures 22 x 38 inches. Height, 30 inches.

R 398 G   Reed Table

For use in living rooms, sun parlors, etc. Wood top and shelf. The top measures 31 x 24 inches. Height, 28½ inches.

R 840 G   Reed Table

An extremely simple, yet attractive, reed end or coffee table. The top measures 21 x 14 inches. It is 22 inches high.

R 842 G   Reed Table

A handy, well made reed table of Moderne design. The top measures 28 x 14½ inches. It is 22 inches high.

R 841 G   Reed Table

An end, console or wall reed table, designed in the Moderne manner. The top measures 30 x 13 inches. It is 22 inches high.

R 808 G   Fibre Table

An unusual wood and fibre table that has many uses. The top measures 36 x 24 inches. It is 30 inches high.

For Finishes See Page 5

R 649 G   Fibre Table

An octagonal-top table for use in living rooms, sun parlors, etc. The top measures 30 inches across. It is 30 inches high.

R 689 G   Reed Table

A reed table of unique design with a wood top which measures 20 x 18 inches. It is 30 inches high.

R 811 G   Fibre Table

A good-looking table for use in almost any room. The top measures 34 x 24 inches. It is 30 inches high.

R 9851 G   Reed and Fibre Table

An attractive table with wood top and lower shelf. The top measures 42 x 18 inches. Height, 29 inches.

R 539 G   Fibre Table

A graceful, round table woven of fibre. The top is 30 inches in diameter. The table is 30 inches high.

R 627 G   Rattan Table

This table looks especially well with reed furniture. It has a removable glass-bottom tray. Top, 20 x 30 inches. Height, 29 inches.

R 641 G   Reed Table

The oval top measures 20 x 30 inches. Height of Table, 30 inches.

R 814 G   Fibre Table

An attractive fibre table for use in almost any room. The top measures 30 x 20 inches. It is 30 inches high.

For Finishes See Page 5

R 410 GM   Reed Table

An inexpensive reed table of pleasing design. Diameter of top, 26 inches. Height, 28 inches.

R 410 GS   Reed Table

A smaller size of the table shown at the left. Diameter of top, 22 inches. Height, 28 inches.

R 690 G   Reed Table

A reed table with a wood top and shelf. Top measures 34 x 18 inches. It is 30 inches high.

R 378 G   Reed Table

This table looks well with any reed suite. Diameter of top, 30 inches. Height, 30 inches.

R 825 G   Fibre Table

A fibre table of good design with an attractively shaped top which measures 34 x 22 inches. It is 30 inches high.

R 675 G   Fibre Table

A good-looking fibre table which can be used in almost any room. The top measures 32 x 16 inches. It is 30 inches high.

R 691 GL   Reed Table

An attractive reed table. The top measures 34 x 20 inches. It is 30 inches high.

R 691 GS   Reed Table

The smaller size of the table shown at the left. Top, 30 x 15 inches. Height, 30 inches.

For Finishes See Page 5

R 447 G   Reed Table

An attractive, inexpensive table woven of
reed. The round wood top is 26 inches in
diameter. The table is 30 inches high.

R 824 G   Fibre Table

An inexpensive, but good-looking, fibre table with
a rectangular top which measures 28 x 30 inches.
It is 30 inches high.

R 9653 G   Reed Table

For use in living rooms and libraries
as end or console table. Width over
all, 12 inches. Length over all, 24
inches. Height, 26 inches.

R 637 G   Fibre Table

This table may be used as davenport
end or console table. Top measures
25 x 12 inches. Height, 24½ inches.

R 590 G   Fibre Table

A fibre table for use as a console
table or at ends of davenports. The
wood top measures 23½ x 13½
inches. Height is 24 inches.

R 688 G   Reed Table

A small end table for use with davenports,
arm chairs, etc. Top, 24 x 12 inches. Height,
24½ inches.

R 665 G   Fibre Table

An occasional or end table with a wood top
which measures 24 x 12 inches. It is 24½
inches high.

R 702 GS   Reed Table

A small table which may be used in living
rooms, sun parlors, etc. Top, 9½ x 20
inches. Height, 24 inches.

For Finishes See Page 5

R 672 G   Fibre Table

An occasional or end table with a book
trough. The wood top measures 24 x 12
inches. It is 24½ inches high.

R 673 G   Reed Table

An oblong-shaped table with a wood top and book
trough. Top measures 24 x 12 inches. It is 24½
inches high.

R 687 G   Reed Table

A small end table with a book trough. The
top measures 24 x 12 inches. It is 24½
inches high.

R 630   Fibre Serving Table

An attractive fibre serving table with cabinet. The wood top measures 36 x 16½
inches. It is 32 inches high.

R 631 G   Fibre Extension Table

A two-leaf extension table. Size closed, 45 x 26½
inches. Size extended 1 leaf, 45 x 34½ inches. Size
extended 2 leaves, 45 x 42½ inches. Height, 30
inches.

R 406 G   Reed Table

(Shown with R 406 A chairs.) Has wood
top, 42 inches in diameter. The table is 30
inches high.

R 413 G   Reed Table

(Shown with R 413 A chairs.) The wood
top is 36 inches in diameter. The table is 30
inches high.

For Finishes See Page 5

R 9825 W   Fibre Desk

A distinctive fibre desk with attractively shaped wood top, 32 inches long, 20 inches wide. Height, 29 inches. Equipped with electric light fixture.

R 491 W   Fibre Desk

A handsome fibre desk of graceful design. The top measures 36 x 24 inches. The desk is 30 inches in height.

R 702 W   Reed Desk

A graceful desk of unique design. Top measures 22 x 38 inches. It is 29 inches high.

R 192 W   Reed Desk

(Shown with R 192 A chair) A woven reed desk with wood top. The length over all is 37 inches; width over all, 22 inches; height, 30 inches.

R 9669 W   Fibre Desk

An attractive fibre desk with wood top. Fitted with reed wastepaper basket. Dimensions of top, 32½ x 21 inches. Height, 29 inches.

For Finishes See Page 5

R 417   Reed Tea Wagon

A well-designed tea wagon woven of reed. Has removable glass-bottom tray. Equipped with rubber tired casters and wood wheels. The tray measures 22 x 14 inches.

R 9045 W   **Reed Desk**

A serviceable desk woven of reed. Has two side drawers. Dimensions of top, 28 x 17 inches. Height of desk, 30 inches.

R 91 W   **Reed Desk**

An attractive desk woven of reed. Made with lifting lid. The top measures 28½ x 16½ inches. The desk is 29 inches high.

R 674 W   **Reed Desk**

A graceful looking desk woven of reed with a wood top. The top measures 36 x 16 inches. It is 30 inches high.

R 808 W   **Fibre Desk**

An attractive fibre desk. The top measures 28 x 18 inches. It is 30 inches high.

R 810 W   **Fibre Desk**

A newly designed desk woven of fibre. The top measures 30 x 20 inches. It is 30 inches high.

R 655 W   **Fibre Desk**

This inexpensive fibre desk is suitable for use with many different furniture combinations. The top measures 20 x 32 inches. The height is 29 inches.

R 702   **Reed Fernery**

A fernery for use in almost any room. Has self-watering pan. Height, 33 inches. Over-all measurements, 12 x 30 inches.

For Finishes See Page 5

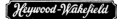

R 260
Reed
Bird Cage
Diameter, 8 in.
Height, 20 in.

R 416   Reed Fernery

A reed fernery of pleasing design. Has self-watering pan. The inside measurements are 28 x 10 inches. (Bird cage priced extra.) Height over all, 68 inches.

R 583 L   Fibre Fernery

An attractively woven fibre fernery with self-watering pan. This fernery is 35 inches long, 11 inches wide, 7 inches deep, and 30 inches high.

R 583 S   Fibre Fernery

The smaller size of the fernery shown at the left. 24 inches long, 11 inches wide, 7 inches deep, and 30 inches high. Has self-watering pan.

R 540   Reed Fernery

A reed fernery of striking design. It has a self-watering pan. Height, 32 inches. Over-all measurements, 10 x 30 inches.

R 367 L   Reed Fernery

A good-selling fernery woven of reed. Has self-watering pan. This fernery is 36 inches long, 11½ inches wide, and 7 inches deep. It stands 30 inches high.

For Finishes See Page 5

R 367 S   Reed Fernery

The smaller size of the fernery shown at the left. Has self-watering pan, 25 inches long, 11½ inches wide, 7 inches deep, and 30 inches high.

R 686 Reed Fernery

A reed fernery with a self-watering pan. Over-all dimensions, 36 x 11½ inches. Height, 30 inches.

R 586 L Reed Fernery

A reasonably priced fernery woven of reed. Has self-watering pan, 7 inches deep. Dimensions over all, 35 x 11 inches. Height, 30 inches.

R 586 S Reed Fernery

The smaller size of the fernery shown at the left. Equipped with self-watering pan, 7 inches deep. Dimensions over all, 24 x 11 inches. Height, 30 inches.

R 645 Fibre Fernery

Equipped with removable pan, 9 inches deep. Outside dimensions, 28 x 12 inches. Height, 30 inches.

R 9785 Fibre Fernery

A fernery woven of fibre. Has self-watering pan, 6 inches deep. Length over all, 31 inches. Width over all, 10 inches. Height, 31 inches.

R 710 Reed Fernery

An attractive fernery woven of reed. Equipped with removable pan 7¾ inches deep. Outside dimensions are 11 x 30 inches. The height is 30 inches.

R 657 Reed Fernery

A well-designed yet inexpensive reed fernery, with removable pan 4 inches deep. Outside dimensions, 9½ x 30 inches. Height, 30 inches.

For Finishes See Page 5

R 441   Reed Plant Stand

A striking plant stand woven of reed. The basket at top is **9** inches in diameter, and **9** inches deep. This stand is **38** inches high.

R 573   Reed Plant Stand

An attractive plant stand woven of reed. The removable basket is **11** inches in diameter and **10** inches deep. The stand is **33** inches high, over all.

R 646   Fibre Fernery

Same as R 645, but shorter. Equipped with removable pan, **9** inches deep. Outside dimensions, **12 x 12** inches. Height, **30** inches.

**R 322
Reed Tabouret**

A well-designed tabouret woven of reed. Has octagonal reed top, **13½** inches in diameter. This tabouret is **20** inches high.

R 837   Fibre Tabouret

An attractive tabouret with a top which measures **13½ x 13½** inches. It is **20** inches high.

R 9590   Reed Standard

A graceful standard woven of reed for use with bird cage or hanging plant. This standard is **72** inches high.

**R 530
Reed Waste-
Paper Basket**

The diameter of the waste-paper basket is **13** inches. Height, **13** inches.

**R 9120
Reed Basket**

Diameter, **10½** inches. Height, **14** inches.

R 591   Fibre Book Case

An attractive book case woven of fibre. Has four wood shelves which measure **20 x 10** inches. The book case is **42** inches high.

**R 7672
Reed Wood Basket**

An attractive basket woven of reed, **20** inches long and **13** inches wide.

**R 210
Reed Wood Basket**

A low-priced, serviceable wood basket, woven of reed, **20** inches long and **13** inches wide.

For Finishes See Page 5

R 502 E   Table Lamp

An artistic table lamp woven of reed. Fitted for two electric lights. Shade of silk or cretonne, as desired. Diameter of shade, 17 inches. Height of lamp, 21 inches.

**R 9720
Reed Smoker's
Stand**

A graceful smoker woven of reed fitted with tray. Height, 26½ inches.

**R 395
Reed Smoker's Stand**

Another attractive smoker's stand wound with reed. The diameter of the top shelf is 9 inches. The height over all is 37 inches.

(Ash tray and humidor not furnished.)

**R 396
Reed Smoker's Stand**

This simple, but attractive, smoker's stand is wound with reed. The wood top measures 13 x 13 inches. Height of stand, 28½ inches.

**R 198
Reed Costumer**

72 inches high.

R 734 E   Table Lamp

This modernistic table lamp is woven of stick reed and is fitted for one electric light. The shade is made of Crystaline. The overall width of the shade is 11 inches. Height of the lamp is 23½ inches.

R 529 E   Table Lamp

A graceful table lamp woven of fibre. Fitted for two electric lights. The fibre shade is ornamented with silk fringe. Diameter of shade, 18½ inches. Height of lamp, 24 inches.

R 375 E   Table Lamp

A well-designed table lamp woven of reed. Fitted for one electric light. The shade is 15 inches in diameter, and may be lined with cretonne or silk, as desired. The lamp is 24 inches high.

R 8263 E   Table Lamp

A reasonably priced table lamp woven of reed. Fitted for one electric light. Shade lined with cretonne or silk, as desired. Diameter of shade, 14 inches. Height of lamp, 21 inches.

R 555 E   Table Lamp

An attractive table lamp woven of fibre. Fitted for two electric lights. The shade is trimmed with silk fringe and is 18½ inches in diameter. The lamp is 23 inches high.

For Finishes See Page 5

R 361 E   Floor Lamp

This lamp, woven of reed, is 69 inches high. It is fitted for two electric lights. The shade is lined with cretonne or silk as desired. Diameter of shade, 27 inches.

R 579 E   Floor Lamp

An attractive floor lamp woven of fibre and fitted for two electric lights. The shade is of fibre, with silk fringe. Diameter of shade, 21½ inches. Height of lamp, 62 inches.

R 556 E   Floor Lamp

An attractive floor lamp woven of fibre and fitted for two electric lights. The shade is of fibre with silk fringe. The diameter of the shade is 22½ inches. The lamp is 60 inches high.

R 581 E   Bridge Lamp

A graceful bridge lamp woven of fibre. Fitted for one electric light. The shade is of fibre trimmed with silk fringe. The diameter of the shade is 13 inches. The lamp is 59 inches high.

R 578 E   Bridge Lamp

A distinctive-looking bridge lamp woven of reed. Fitted for one electric light. The shade is of silk and is 11 inches in diameter. The lamp is 60 inches high.

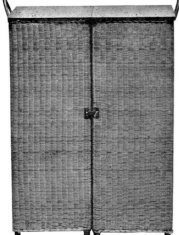

R 585   Infant's Fibre Wardrobe

A roomy infant's wardrobe made of fibre. When closed, the top of this wardrobe measures 23 x 16 inches. The left side of the wardrobe has rod for clothes hangers, and removable shelf. The wardrobe is 32 inches high.

R 597   Fibre Hampers

These well-made hampers are woven of fibre. The small size measures 13 inches long, 8 inches wide, and 23 inches deep. The medium size is 16 x 10 x 23 inches. The large size measures 20 x 12 x 23 inches.

For Finishes See Page 5

R 851 Fibre Crib

This is a good-looking fibre crib with woven diamond designs on all sides. The crib is 42½ inches long and 24 inches wide.

R 400 Reed Crib

This attractive crib is woven of reed. It has a spring bottom and a drop side (as shown). The crib is 42½ inches long and 24 inches wide.

R 516 Reed Bassinet

An attractive bassinet woven of reed. Has three canopy bows. The inside measurements are 30 x 13 inches.

R 150
Reed Cabinet

Width between Arms, 10½ inches. Depth of Seat, 9 inches. Height of Back, 12 inches.

R 517
Reed Cabinet
Fitted with Rubber Ring, Wire and Chamber

Width between Arms, 11 inches. Depth of Seat, 10½ inches. Height of Back, 13½ inches.

R 550
Reed Cabinet
Fitted with Chamber Wires

Width between Arms, 11 inches. Depth of Seat, 11 inches. Height of Back, 15½ inches.

R 850 N
Youth's Fibre Rocker
with Box Cushion

Width between Arms, 14½ inches. Depth of Seat, 14 inches. Height of Back, 15 inches.

R 9766 H
Reed High Chair

Chair is shown with wood shelf, which can be furnished with Enamel or Aluminum Tray. Width between Arms, 12 inches. Depth of Seat, 12 inches. Height of Back, 14 inches.

For Finishes See Page 5

R 205 N
Child's Reed Rocker
Width between Arms, 12
inches. Depth of Seat, 11
inches. Height of Back, 18
inches.

R 551 K
Child's Reed Chair
with Box Cushion
Width between Arms, 13
inches. Depth of Seat, 12
inches. Height of Back, 14
inches.

R 551 N
Child's Reed Rocker
with Box Cushion
Width between Arms, 13
inches. Depth of Seat, 12
inches. Height of Back, 14
inches.

R 346 N
Child's Reed Rocker
with Box Cushion
Width between Arms, 13
inches. Depth of Seat, 13
inches. Height of Back,
15½ inches.

R 593 N
Child's Fibre Rocker
Width between Arms, 12
inches. Depth of Seat, 12½
inches. Height of Back,
15½ inches.

R 848 N
Child's Fibre Rocker
with Box Cushion
Width between Arms, 10½
inches. Depth of Seat, 12
inches. Height of Back, 12½
inches.

R 813 N
Child's Fibre Rocker
Pad Cushion. Width be-
tween Arms, 12 inches. Depth
of Seat, 12 inches. Height
of Back, 13½ inches.

R 642 N
Child's Fibre Rocker
with Pad Seat
Width between Arms, 13½
inches. Depth of Seat, 13½
inches. Height of Back, 14
inches.

R 643 N
Child's Fibre Rocker
with Pad Seat
Width between Arms, 13½
inches. Depth of Seat, 13½
inches. Height of Back, 17
inches.

R 644 N
Child's Fibre Rocker
with Pad Seat
Width between Arms, 13½
inches. Depth of Seat, 13½
inches. Height of Back, 17
inches.

For Finishes See Page 5

R 599   Child's Reed Wheel Chair

		Inches
Height of Back from Seat	. . . . .	21
Height of Seat from Floor	. . . .	21½
Height of Seat from Foot Rest	. . .	13
Height of Arms from Seat	. . . .	7½
Depth of Seat	. . . .	14
Width between Arms	. . . . .	15
Diameter of Large Wheels	. . . .	22
Diameter of Small Wheels	. . . .	10
Width Over All	. . . .	24½

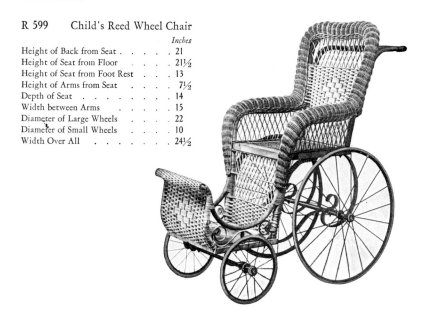

R 2295   Reed Wheel Chair

		Inches
Height of Back from Seat	. . . . .	24½
Height of Seat from Floor	. . . .	19
Height of Seat from Foot Rest	. . .	16¼
Height of Arms from Seat	. . . .	10½
Depth of Seat	. . . .	19½
Width between Arms	. . . . .	18
Diameter of Large Wheels	. . . .	24
Diameter of Small Wheels	. . . .	8
Width Over All	. . . .	27

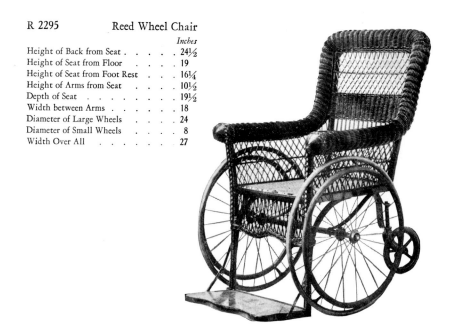

R 600   Reed Wheel Chair

		Inches
Height of Back from Seat	. . . .	24
Height of Seat from Floor	. . . .	23
Height of Seat from Foot Rest	. . .	15
Height of Arms from Seat	. . . .	10
Depth of Seat	. . . . . .	16
Width between Arms	. . . . .	18½
Diameter of Large Wheels	. . . .	24
Diameter of Small Wheels	. . . .	10
Width Over All	. . . .	26½

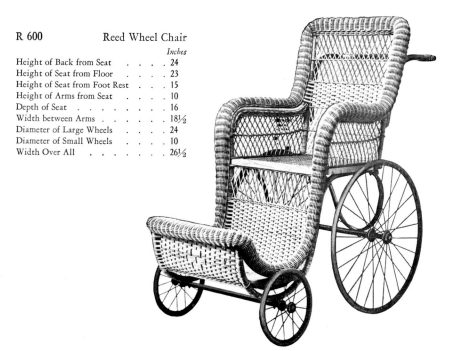

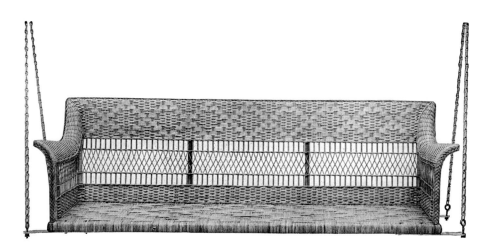

R 203   Reed Swing

An attractive swing woven of Reed. The Seat is 69 inches wide, and 23 inches deep. The Back is 20½ inches high.

Heywood-Wakefield
Direct Factory Shipment Suites

❧

THE reed and fibre furniture shown on this and the next seven pages has been designed for direct shipment from our Gardner, Wakefield, or Chicago factories.

Because of the tremendous volume of production on these pieces, we are able to price them exceptionally low for furniture of this high quality. The specially selected finishes supplied are given for each pattern   They can be upholstered in cretonne or tapestry.

If you will send your order to the warehouse with which you usually trade, shipment will be arranged from the nearest factory.

R 830-60   Fibre Davenport

Removable Spring Cushion. Width between Arms, 60 inches.
Depth of Seat, 23 inches. Height of Back, 17 inches.

R 830 C   Fibre Chair

Removable Spring Cushion. Width between
Arms, 18½ inches. Depth of Seat, 20 inches.
Height of Back, 17 inches.

FINISHES—Sand, Decorated; Dark Brown, Decorated; Burnt Orange, Decorated; Green Gold, Decorated; Lavender Gold, Decorated; and Fallow, Decorated (a new and popular light brown type of finish)

These patterns are shipped direct from our factories at Gardner, Mass., or Chicago, Ill.

R 830 D   Fibre Rocker

Removable Spring Cushion. Width between
Arms, 18½ inches. Depth of Seat, 20 inches.
Height of Back, 17 inches.

R 670 C Fibre Chair

Removable Spring Cushion. Width between
Arms, 19 inches. Depth of Seat, 20 inches.
Height of Back, 17 inches.

R 670-60 Fibre Davenport

Removable Spring Cushion. Width between Arms, 60 inches.
Depth of Seat, 22 inches. Height of Back, 17 inches.

R 670 D Fibre Rocker

Removable Spring Cushion. Width between
Arms, 19 inches. Depth of Seat, 20 inches.
Height of Back, 17 inches.

FINISHES—Sand, Decorated; Dark Brown, Decorated; Burnt
Orange, Decorated; Green Gold, Decorated; Lavender Gold,
Decorated; and Fallow, Decorated (a new and popular light
brown type of finish).

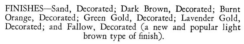

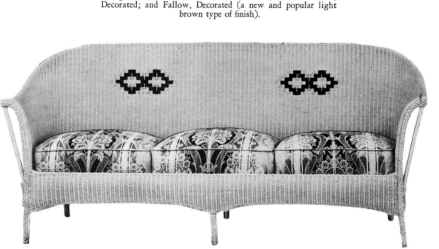

R 680 C Fibre Chair

Removable Spring Cushion. Width between
Arms, 19½ inches. Depth of Seat, 20 inches.
Height of Back, 18 inches.

R 680-60 Fibre Davenport

Removable Spring Cushion. Width between Arms, 60 inches.
Depth of Seat, 22 inches. Height of Back, 18 inches.

R 680-48 Fibre Settee

This pattern is the same as the one shown above, but shorter.
Removable Spring Cushion. Width between Arms, 48 inches.
Depth of Seat, 22 inches. Height of Back, 18 inches.

R 680 D Fibre Rocker

Removable Spring Cushion. Width between Arms, 19½ inches. Depth of Seat, 20
inches. Height of Back, 18 inches.

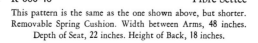

These patterns are shipped direct from our factories at Gardner,
Mass., or Chicago, Ill.

R 669 C   Fibre Chair

Removable Spring Cushion. Width between Arms, 19 inches. Depth of Seat, 20 inches. Height of Back, 20 inches.

R 669-60   Fibre Davenport

Removable Spring Cushion. Width between Arms, 60 inches. Depth of Seat, 22 inches. Height of Back, 20 inches.

R 669 D   Fibre Rocker

Removable Spring Cushion. Width between Arms, 19 inches. Depth of Seat, 20 inches. Height of Back, 20 inches.

FINISHES—Sand, Decorated; Dark Brown, Decorated; Burnt Orange, Decorated; Green Gold, Decorated; Lavender Gold, Decorated; and Fallow, Decorated (a new and popular light brown type of finish).

R 669-48   Fibre Settee

Removable Spring Cushion. Width between Arms, 48 inches. Depth of Seat, 22 inches. Height of Back, 20 inches.

R 669 J   Fibre Chaise Longue

Removable Spring Cushion. Width between Arms, 21 inches. Length of Seat, 52 inches. Height of Back, 19 inches.

These patterns are shipped direct from our factories at Gardner, Mass., or Chicago, Ill.

R 829 C   Fibre Chair

Removable Spring Cushion. Width between Arms, 18½ inches. Depth of Seat, 20 inches. Height of Back, 19 inches.

R 829-60   Fibre Davenport

Removable Spring Cushion. Width between Arms, 60 inches. Depth of Seat, 23 inches. Height of Back, 19 inches.

R 829 D   Fibre Rocker

Removable Spring Cushion. Width between Arms, 18½ inches. Depth of Seat, 20 inches. Height of Back, 19 inches.

FINISHES—Sand, Decorated; Dark Brown, Decorated; Burnt Orange, Decorated; Green Gold, Decorated; Lavender Gold, Decorated; and Fallow, Decorated (a new and popular light brown type of finish).

R 831 C   Fibre Chair

Removable Spring Cushion. Width between Arms, 18½ inches. Depth of Seat, 20 inches. Height of Back, 25 inches.

R 831-60   Fibre Davenport

Removable Spring Cushion. Width between Arms, 60 inches. Depth of Seat, 23 inches. Height of Back, 25 inches.

R 831 D   Fibre Rocker

Removable Spring Cushion. Width between Arms, 18½ inches. Depth of Seat, 20 inches. Height of Back, 25 inches.

These patterns are shipped direct from our factories at Gardner, Mass., or Chicago, Ill.

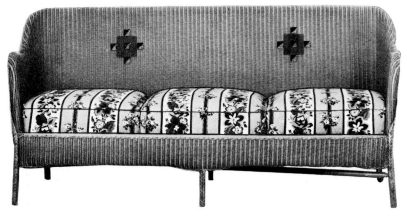

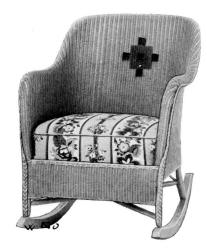

R 634-60 Fibre Davenport

Removable Spring Cushion. Width between Arms, 60 inches. Depth of Seat, 23 inches. Height of Back, 17 inches.

R 634-48 Fibre Settee

This pattern is the same as the one shown above, but shorter. Removable Spring Cushion. Width between Arms, 48 inches. Depth of Seat, 23 inches. Height of Back, 17 inches.

FINISHES—Sand, Decorated; Dark Brown, Decorated; Burnt Orange, Decorated; Green Gold, Decorated; Lavender Gold, Decorated; and Fallow, Decorated (a new and popular light brown type of finish).

R 634 C Fibre Chair

Removable Spring Cushion. Width between Arms, 18½ inches. Depth of Seat, 20 inches. Height of Back, 17 inches.

Fibre Rocker

Removable Spring Cushion. Width between Arms, 18½ inches. Depth of Seat, 20 inches. Height of Back, 17 inches.

R 832-42 Fibre Settee

Removable Box Cushion over Springs. Width between Arms, 42 inches. Depth of Seat, 20 inches. Height of Back, 19 inches.

FINISHES—Sand; Waverly (a light green); and Fallow (a light brown).

R 832 C Fibre Chair

Removable Box Cushion over Springs. Width between Arms, 18½ inches. Depth of Seat, 18 inches. Height of Back, 19 inches.

R 832 D Fibre Rocker

Removable Box Cushion over Springs. Width between Arms, 18½ inches. Depth of Seat, 18 inches. Height of Back, 19 inches.

These patterns are shipped direct from our factories at Gardner, Mass., or Chicago, Ill.

R 732 C   Reed Chair

Removable Spring Cushion. Width between
Arms, 19½ inches. Depth of Seat, 19½
inches. Height of Back, 24 inches.

R 732-60   Reed Davenport

Removable Spring Cushion. Width between Arms, 60 inches.
Depth of Seat, 24 inches. Height of Back, 24 inches.

FINISHES—Sand; Dark Brown; Fallow (a light brown); Waverly (a light green); Flamingo (a rose gold); Chinese Orange;
and Chinese Green.

R 732 D   Reed Rocker

Removable Spring Cushion. Width between
Arms, 19½ inches. Depth of Seat, 19½
inches. Height of Back, 24 inches.

R 728 C   Reed Chair

Removable Spring Cushion. Width between
Arms, 19½ inches. Depth of Seat, 19½
inches. Height of Back, 25 inches.

R 728-60   Reed Davenport

Removable Spring Cushion. Width between Arms, 60 inches.
Depth of Seat, 24 inches. Height of Back, 24 inches.

These patterns are shipped direct from our factories at Wakefield,
Mass., or Chicago, Ill.

R 728 D   Reed Rocker

Removable Spring Cushion. Width between
Arms, 19½ inches. Depth of Seat, 19½
inches. Height of Back, 25 inches.

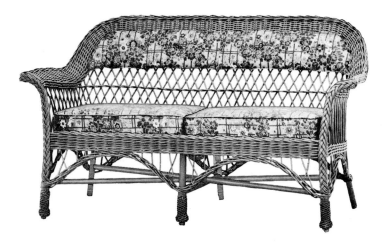

R 550 C   Reed Chair

Removable Spring Cushion. Width between Arms, 18 inches. Depth of Seat, 19 inches. Height of Back, 19 inches.

R 550-48   Reed Settee

Removable Spring Cushion. Width between Arms, 48 inches. Depth of Seat, 22 inches. Height of Back, 18 inches.

R 550 D   Reed Rocker

Removable Spring Cushion. Width between Arms, 18 inches. Depth of Seat, 19 inches. Height of Back, 19 inches.

FINISHES—Sand; Dark Brown; Fallow (a light brown); Waverly (a light green); Flamingo (a rose gold); Chinese Orange; and Chinese Green.

R 713-48   Reed Settee

Removable Spring Cushion. Width between Arms, 48 inches. Depth of Seat, 22 inches. Height of Back, 19 inches.

R 713 C   Reed Chair

Removable Spring Cushion. Width between Arms, 18½ inches. Depth of Seat, 19½ inches. Height of Back, 19 inches.

R 713 D   Reed Rocker

Removable Spring Cushion. Width between Arms, 18½ inches. Depth of Seat, 19½ inches. Height of Back, 19 inches.

These patterns are shipped direct from our factories at Wakefield, Mass., or Chicago, Ill.

R 848 N
Child's Fibre Rocker

Width between Arms, 10½ inches. Depth of Seat, 12 inches. Height of Back, 12½ inches.

R 824 G — Fibre Table

The top measures 28 x 30 inches. The table is 30 inches high.

R 612 G — Fibre Table

The top measures 30 x 20 inches. The table is 30 inches high.

R 836 — Fibre Fernery

Outside dimensions, 30½ x 10 inches. Equipped with removable pan 4 inches deep. The fernery is 30 inches high.

The four patterns shown above can be furnished in Sand, Dark Brown, Burnt Orange, Green Gold, Lavender Gold or Fallow finishes.

R 733 N
Child's Reed Rocker

Width between Arms, 12 inches. Depth of Seat, 11½ inches. Height of Back, 12½ inches.

This child's stick reed rocker is woven of pre-colored reeds and is supplied only in Artone finish—an attractive combination of orange and brown reeds hand-woven over a light green frame.

R 814 G — Fibre Table

The top measures 30 x 20 inches. The table is 30 inches high.

The above table can be furnished in the following finishes: Sand, Decorated; Dark Brown, Decorated; Burnt Orange, Decorated; Green Gold, Decorated; Lavender Gold, Decorated; and Fallow, Decorated.

R 641 G — Reed Table

The top measures 30 x 20 inches. The table is 30 inches high.

R 553 G — Reed Table

The top measures 21 x 31 inches. The table is 30 inches high.

These two tables can be furnished in the following finishes: Sand; Dark Brown; Fallow; Waverly; Flamingo; Chinese Orange; and Chinese Green.

These patterns are shipped direct from our factories at Gardner, Mass., Wakefield, Mass., or Chicago, Ill.

HEYWOOD-WAKEFIELD

WOOD Furniture

Comfort

This de luxe Coxwell, C 3026 C (page 88), affords
genuine comfort because of its deep, spring-
filled back and seat cushion, and upholstered arms. It is shown in Antique
Walnut with etched mohair on the
sides and arms, and a beautiful,
heavy velour on the back
and seat, both 8 grade
upholsteries. The
gateleg end table
is C 3023 G
(page 90).

C 3015 C
Sag Seat
Height of Back, 20 in.
Width between Arms, 24 in.

C 3016-60
Reversible Spring Filled Seat Cushions
Height of Back, 20 in.
Width between Arms, 60 in.

C 3016 C
Reversible Spring
Filled Seat Cushion
Height of Back, 20 in.
Width between Arms, 26 in.

C 3014 C
Sag Seat
Height of Back, 18½ in.
Width between Arms, 23½ in.

C 3012–64
Spring Filled Seat Cushions
Height of Back, 19 in.
Width between Arms, 64 in.

C 3012 C
Spring Filled Seat Cushion
Height of Back, 19½ in.
Width between Arms, 25 in.

For Finishes See Price List

C 3025 C
Upholstered Spring Seat and Back
Height of Back,   25 in.
Width between Arms, 22 in.

C 3026 C
Upholstered Spring Seat and Back
Height of Back,   25 in.
Width between Arms, 23 in.

C 3045 C
Upholstered Spring Seat and Back
Height of Back,   28 in.
Width between Arms, 20 in.

C 3044 C
Upholstered Spring Seat and Back
Height of Back,   27 in.
Width between Arms, 21 in.

C 3042 C
Upholstered Spring Seat and Back
Height of Back,   24 in.
Width between Arms, 22 in.

C 1513 C
Upholstered Spring Seat
and Back
Height of Back,   21 in.
Width between Arms, 21 in.

C 3015 CX
Sag Seat
Height of Back,   20 in.
Width between Arms, 24 in.

C 3047 C
Sag Seat
Height of Back,   19 in.
Width between Arms, 19 in.

For Finishes See Price List

C 3050 C
Sag Seat
Height of Back,   21 in.
Width between Arms, 19 in.

C 3048 C
Sag Seat
Height of Back,   21 in.
Width between Arms, 19 in.

C 433 C
Sag Seat
Height of Back,   18½ in.
Width between Arms, 22½ in.

C 433 D
Sag Seat
Height of Back,   18½ in.
Width between Arms, 22½ in.

C 422 D
Removable Spring Seat
Height of Back,   21½ in.
Width between Arms, 19½ in.

C 423 D
Removable Spring Seat
Height of Back,   21½ in.
Width between Arms, 19½ in.

C 424 D
Removable Spring Seat
Height of Back,   22½ in.
Width between Arms, 19½ in.

C 403 D
Removable Spring Seat
Height of Back,   22¼ in.
Width between Arms, 18½ in.

For Finishes See Price List

C 5054 C
Removable Spring Seat
Height of Back,   19 in.
Width between Arms, 20 in.

C 1492 G
Top, 30 x 30 in.
Height,   29 in.

C 1489 G
Top, 24 x 10 in.
Height,   26 in.

C 5054 D
Removable Spring Seat
Height of Back,   19 in.
Width between Arms, 20 in.

C 5058 C
Sag Seat
Height of Back,   21 in.
Width between Arms, 20½ in.

C 3023 G
Top, open,   24 x 20 in.
Top, closed,   24 x 10 in.
Height,   26 in.

C 3023 G
The above illustration shows the
table with the leaf down.

C 5058 D
Sag Seat
Height of Back,   20 in.
Width between Arms, 20½ in.

For Finishes See Price List

C 5057 C
Removable Spring Seat
Height of Back,   18½ in.
Width between Arms, 20   in.

C 3027
Upholstered Spring Seat
Height,   14 in.
Top, 22 x 18 in.

C 3028
Upholstered Spring Seat
Height,   14 in.
Top, 22 x 18 in.

C 5057 D
Removable Spring Seat
Height of Back,   18½ in.
Width between Arms, 20   in.

C 5061 C
Sag Seat
Height of Back,   20   in.
Width between Arms, 20½ in.

C 2034
Height,   8 in.
Top,   14 x 9 in.

C 2035
Height,   10 in.
Top,   16 x 10 in.

C 1495
Inside Dimensions, 26 x 9½ in.
Height,   30 in.

C 5061 D
Sag Seat
Height of Back,   20   in.
Width between Arms, 20½ in.

For Finishes See Price List

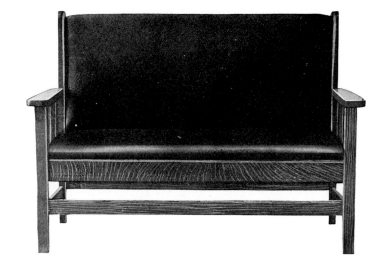

C 758-51 X
Back and Spring Seat
Upholstered in Leather
Height of Back,   24½ in.
Width between Arms, 51   in.
Width Over All,   57½ in.

C 758 CX
Back and Spring Seat
Upholstered in Leather
Height of Back,   24   in.
Width between Arms, 21½ in.

C 758 DX
Back and Spring Seat
Upholstered in Leather
Height of Back,   24   in.
Width between Arms, 21½ in.

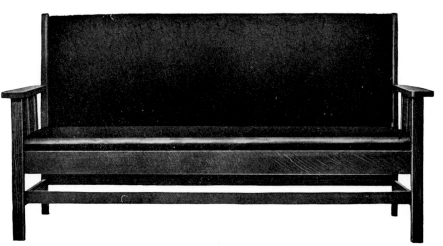

C 758-69 X
Back and Spring Seat
Upholstered in Leather
Height of Back,   24½ in.
Width between Arms, 69   in.
Width Over All,   76   in.

For Finishes See Price List

C 758-51
Spring Seat Upholstered
in Leather
Height of Back,   24½ in.
Width between Arms, 51   in.
Width Over All,   57½ in.

C 758 C
Spring Seat Upholstered
in Leather
Height of Back,   24   in.
Width between Arms, 21½ in.

C 758 D
Spring Seat Upholstered
in Leather
Height of Back,   24   in.
Width between Arms, 21½ in.

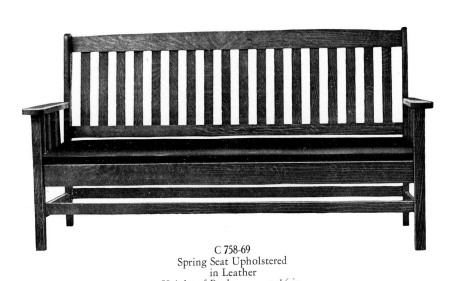

C 758-69
Spring Seat Upholstered
in Leather
Height of Back,   24½ in.
Width between Arms, 69   in.
Width Over All,   76   in.

For Finishes See Price List

C 242-70
Saddle Seat
Height of Back,   20 in.
Width between Arms, 70 in.
Width Over All,   78 in.

C 242 A
Saddle Seat
Height of Back, 19½ in.
Width of Seat,   18½ in.

C 242 D
Saddle Seat
Height of Back,   20 in.
Width between Arms, 18 in.

C 242 C
Saddle Seat
Height of Back,   20 in.
Width between Arms, 18 in.

For Finishes See Price List

C 1121 A
Saddle Seat
Height of Back, 20½ in.
Width of Seat, 17½ in.

C 1121 C
Saddle Seat
Height of Back, 23½ in.
Width between Arms, 19½ in.

C 1121 D
Saddle Seat
Height of Back, 23½ in.
Width between Arms, 19½ in.

C 1121-46½
Saddle Seat
Height of Back, 24 in.
Width between Arms, 46½ in.
Width Over All, 54 in.

C 880 G
Top, 24 x 36 in.
Height, 29 in.

For Finishes See Price List

C 2088 A
Fibre Seat
Height of Back, 19½ in.
Width of Seat, 16 in.

C 2088-40
Fibre Seat
Height of Back, 21½ in.
Width between Arms, 40 in.

C 2088 C
Fibre Seat
Height of Back, 21½ in.
Width between Arms, 19½ in.

C 2060 AF
Fibre Seat
Height of Back, 27¾ in.
Width of Seat, 17¼ in.

C 2026 AF
Fibre Seat
Height of Back, 25¾ in.
Width of Seat, 16½ in.

C 2063 AF
Fibre Seat
Height of Back, 22½ in.
Width of Seat, 17 in.

C 2091 A
Fibre Seat
Height of Back, 18 in.
Width of Seat, 16½ in.

For Finishes See Price List

C 2067 C
Upholstered Seat
Height of Back,   20 in.
Width between Arms, 18 in.

C 2067 A
Upholstered Seat
Height of Back, 19 in.
Width of Seat,   17 in.

C 3051 C
Sag Seat
Height of Back,   27½ in.
Width between Arms, 18 in.

C 3020 A
Sag Seat
Height of Back, 20½ in.
Width of Seat,   17 in.

C 3019 A
Sag Seat
Height of Back, 20½ in.
Width of Seat,   17 in.

C 1199 AF
Fibre Seat
Height of Back, 20 in.
Width of Seat, 16½ in.

C 1306 AF
Fibre Seat
Height of Back, 19 in.
Width of Seat,   16½ in.

C 2092 A
Fibre Seat
Height of Back, 17¼ in.
Width of Seat,   16¾ in.

C 2047 C
Fibre Seat
Height of Back,   24 in.
Width between Arms, 18¾ in.

C 2046 C
Fibre Seat
Height of Back,   23¾ in.
Width between Arms, 18¾ in.

For Finishes See Price List

C 2062 C
Saddle Seat
Height of Back,   21½ in.
Width between Arms, 19¼ in.

C 2061 C
Saddle Seat
Height of Back,   22   in.
Width between Arms, 18¾ in.

C 2030 C
Scoop Seat
Height of Back,   26½ in.
Width between Arms, 20   in.

C 2030 D
Scoop Seat
Height of Back,   26½ in.
Width between Arms, 20   in.

C 2044 C
Saddle Seat
Height of Back,   23¾ in.
Width between Arms, 18¼ in.

C 2044 D
Saddle Seat
Height of Back,   23¾ in.
Width between Arms, 18¼ in.

C 2045 C
Saddle Seat
Height of Back,   24 in.
Width between Arms, 20 in.

C 2045 D
Saddle Seat
Height of Back,   24 in.
Width between Arms, 20 in.

For Finishes See Price List

C 2090 C Saddle Seat Height of Back, 23½ in. Width between Arms, 18¾ in.	**C 2038 C** Saddle Seat Height of Back, 23¾ in. Width between Arms, 18¼ in.	**C 1776 C** Saddle Seat Height of Back, 22 in. Width between Arms, 18½ in.	**C 1776 D** Saddle Seat Height of Back, 22 in. Width between Arms, 18½ in.

C 1511 C Saddle Seat Height of Back, 19 in. Width between Arms, 17 in.	**C 1807 C** Saddle Seat Height of Back, 24½ in. Width between Arms, 17 in.	**C 1807 D** Saddle Seat Height of Back, 24½ in. Width between Arms, 17 in.	**C 3049 A** Scoop Seat Height of Back, 20 in. Width of Seat, 19½ in.

For Finishes See Price List

Good design

Here is a breakfast set of unusually good design that is both attractive and useful. Chairs C 2042 A (page 101), table C 2032 G (page 111), and server C 1510 (page 110), are shown. The finish is No. 146, Decorated, a fawn base color with rich brown shadings and harmonizing decorations.

C 1199 AS
Saddle Seat
Height of Back, 20 in.
Width of Seat, 16 in.

C 1199 C
Saddle Seat
Height of Back, 21 in.
Width between Arms, 16 in.

C 1304 A
Saddle Seat
Height of Back, 20 in.
Width of Seat, 16 in.

C 1301 A
Saddle Seat
Height of Back, 20 in.
Width of Seat, 16 in.

C 581 A
Saddle Seat
Height of Back, 20½ in.
Width of Seat, 16½ in.

C 1326 A
Saddle Seat
Height of Back, 21 in.
Width of Seat, 16½ in.

C 1326 C
Saddle Seat
Height of Back, 23 in.
Width between Arms, 18½ in.

C 1326 D
Saddle Seat
Height of Back, 23 in.
Width between Arms, 18½ in.

C 2042 A
Scoop Seat
Height of Back, 18¾ in.
Width of Seat, 16¾ in.

C 2041 A
Scoop Seat
Height of Back, 18¾ in.
Width of Seat, 16¾ in.

For Finishes See Price List

C 1306 AS
Saddle Seat
Height of Back, 19   in.
Width of Seat, 16½ in.

C 2051 A
Saddle Seat
Height of Back, 20¾ in.
Width of Seat,   16½ in.

C 2080 A
Saddle Seat
Height of Back, 17   in.
Width of Seat,   16½ in.

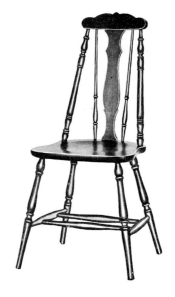

C 2016 A
Scoop Seat
Height of Back, 20   in.
Width of Seat,   16¼ in.

C 2049 A
Scoop Seat
Height of Back, 21½ in.
Width of Seat,   16¾ in.

C 2050 A
Scoop Seat
Height of Back, 21½ in.
Width of Seat,   16¾ in.

C 1801 A
Height of Back, 19 in.
Width of Seat,   17 in.

C 1810 A
Saddle Seat
Height of Back, 19   in.
Width of Seat,   16¾ in.

C 1813 A
Saddle Seat
Height of Back, 18½ in.
Width of Seat,   16¾ in.

C 1814 A
Saddle Seat
Height of Back, 18¾ in.
Width of Seat,   16   in.

For Finishes See Price List

C 1817 A
Saddle Seat
Height of Back,   17¼ in.
Width of Seat,   17¼ in.

C 1819 A
Saddle Seat
Height of Back,   19   in.
Width of Seat,   17¾ in.

C 1816 A
Saddle Seat
Height of Back,   17½ in.
Width of Seat,   17¼ in.

C 124 A SW
Scoop Seat
Wired Back and Understock
Height of Back,   17¾ in.
Width of Seat,   17   in.

C 124 A
Height of Back, 17½ in.
Width of Seat,   16   in.

C 124 AU
Same as above, with Splined Seat.
C 124 AW
Same as C 124 A, but wired around
edge of Seat.

C 1805 A
Height of Back,   17¾ in.
Width of Seat,   15½ in.

C 1455 A
Height of Back,   17½ in.
Width of Seat,   16½ in.

C 1065 A
Height of Back,   18 in.
Width of Seat,   16 in.

C 1830 A
Height of Back,   19   in.
Width of Seat,   15½ in.

C 1831 A
Height of Back,   18   in.
Width of Seat,   15¾ in.

For Finishes See Price List

In the moderne manner

Styled in the Moderne manner, this C 2081 suite (described on the opposite page) brings a new type of beauty to the breakfast room. It is shown in a two-tone green finish with yellow trim, but its unusual design permits the use of many other striking color combinations.

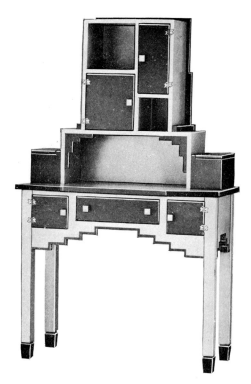

C 2081
Top of Cupboard, 17½ x 40 in.
Total Height,   63 in.

C 2081 C
Height of Back,   20   in.
Width between Arms, 16½ in.

C 2081 A
Height of Back, 20   in.
Width of Seat,   17½ in.

C 2081 G
Top, open,   46 x 36 in.
Top, closed, 36 x 24 in.
Height,   30 in.

For Finishes See Price List

C 3054
Top,   16 x 36 in.
Height,   32 in.

C 3053
Seat,   30 x 14 in.
Height,   18 in.

C 3055 G
Top, open,   64 x 24 in.
Top, closed, 36 x 24 in.
Height,   30 in.

C 3052 A
Saddle Seat
Height of Back, 19½ in.
Width of Seat,   16½ in.

For Finishes See Price List

C 3031
Top, open, 23 x 26½ in.
Top, closed, 14 x 26½ in.
Total Height, 65 in.

C 3029 G
Extension Table
Two Extra Leaves
Top, open, 64 x 32 in.
Top, closed, 48 x 32 in.
Height, 29 in.

C 3030
Top, 50 x 18 in.
Height, 35 in.

C 3032 A
Sag Seat
Height of Back, 20 in.
Width of Seat, 17 in.

For Finishes See Price List

Charm

This colorful set will bring cheerfulness and charm to any breakfast room. The table is our popular C 1 G (page 113) and the chairs, C 1801 A (page 102). The suite is illustrated in a colorful canary yellow finish with fine red striping.

C 1479 A
Upholstered Sag Seat
Height of Back, 18 in.
Width of Seat, 16¼ in.

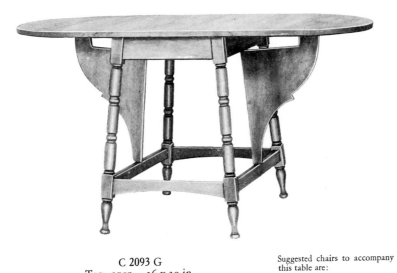

C 2093 G
Top, open, 56 x 30 in.
Top, closed, 30 x 20 in.
Height, 30 in.

Suggested chairs to accompany
this table are:
C 2091 A
C 2063 AF
C 2092 A

C 2093 G
The above illustration shows the
table with the leaves down.

C 1506 A
Slip Seat
Height of Back, 17½ in.
Width of Seat, 15½ in.

C 1493 G
Extension Table
With Extra Leaf
Leaf folds and disappears under top
Top, open, 48½ x 40 in.
Top, closed, 30 x 40 in.
Height, 30 in.

Suggested chairs to accompany
these two tables are:
C 1506 A
C 3020 A
C 3019 A

C 3005 G
Extension Table
Leaves fold neatly under table
Top, open, 53 x 44 in.
Top, closed, 24 x 44 in.
Height, 30 in.

For Finishes See Price List

C 1509
Top, 16½ x 36 in.
Height, 32 in.

C 1508
Top, 16 x 40 in.
Height, 32 in.
Total Height, 64 in.

C 1510
Top of Cupboard, 8½ x 31 in.
Total Height, 58 in.

C 1340
Top, 16½ x 40 in.
Height, 32 in.

C 1315 G
Top, open, 42½ x 36 in.
Top, closed, 22½ x 36 in.
Height, 30 in.

Suggested chairs to accompany this table are:
C 1810 A
C 2049 A
C 2051 A
C 2042 A

C 1320 G
Extension Table
With Extra Leaf
Top, open, 43 x 36 in.
Top, closed, 23 x 36 in.
Top, extended, 55 x 36 in.
Height, 30 in.

Suggested chairs to accompany this table are:
C 1810 A
C 2049 A
C 2051 A
C 2042 A

For Finishes See Price List

C 2036 G

Top, open,   57¾ x 33 in.
Top, closed,   46½ x 33 in.
Height,   29¼ in.

C 2036 G
The illustration above shows the
top extended.

Suggested chairs to accompany C 2036 G and C 2032 G
are:
    C 1199 AS
    C 1326 A
    C 2041 A
    C 2080 A
    C 2050 A
    C 1810 A

C 2032 G

Top, open,   53   x 30 in.
Top, closed,   40¾ x 30 in.
Height,   29¼ in.

C 2032 G
The illustration above shows the
top extended.

C 2064 G

Top, open,   42¼ x 36 in.
Top, closed,   22¼ x 36 in.
Height,   30 in.

Suggested chairs to accompany this table
are: C 1816 A, C 1817 A, C 1813 A, and
C 1801 A.

For Finishes See Price List

Graceful lines

Here is an inexpensive breakfast suite with graceful and attractive lines that has already proved a fast-selling combination. It consists of the C 1 G table (page 113) and the C 1819 A chair (page 103). The finish illustrated is Springtime green with fine gold striping.

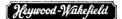

Suggested chairs to accompany this table are:
C 1830 A
C 1816 A
C 1819 A
C 1817 A
C 1814 A
C 1801 A

Suggested chairs to accompany this table are:
C 1817 A
C 1813 A
C 1810 A
C 1801 A
C 2050 A
C 2016 A

C 1 G

Top, open,	42 x 36 in.
Top, closed,	21 x 36 in.
Height,	29½ in.

C 2 G

Top, open,	42 x 36 in.
Top, closed,	21 x 36 in.
Height,	29½ in.

C 2017 G

Top,	36 x 36 in.
Height,	30 in.

C 2018 G

Top,	36 x 36 in.
Height,	30 in.

C 2019 G

Top,	30 x 30 in.
Height,	30 in.

For Finishes See Price List

C 1378 A
Saddle Seat
Bolt Construction
Height of Back,   18½ in.
Width of Seat,   16   in.

C 1378 C
Saddle Seat
Bolt Construction
Height of Back,   29 in.
Width between Arms, 19 in.

C 1378 D
Saddle Seat
Bolt Construction
Height of Back,   29 in.
Width between Arms, 19 in.

C 1294 D
Saddle Seat
Height of Back,   23 in.
Width between Arms, 17 in.

C 1809 D
Saddle Seat
Height of Back,   25¼ in.
Width between Arms, 15¾ in.

C 57 D
Saddle Seat
Height of Back,   25½ in.
Width between Arms, 18½ in.

For Finishes See Price List

C 124 A
Width of Seat, 16 in.
Height of Back, 17½ in.

C 1816 A
Width of Seat, 17¼ in.
Height of Back, 17½ in.

C 1801 A
Width of Seat, 17 in.
Height of Back, 19 in.

C 1455 A
Width of Seat, 16½ in.
Height of Back, 17½ in.

C 957-22½
Width of Seat, 16½ in.
Height of Back, 10½ in.
Height of Seat, 22½ in.

C 2079 A
Width of Seat, 16½ in.
Height of Back, 17½ in.

C 955-24
Diameter of Seat, 13 in.
Height,   24 in.

C 550-17
Diameter of Seat, 14 in.
Height,   17 in.

C 1812 A
Saddle Seat
Height of Back, 19¼ in.
Width of Seat, 16½ in.

C 1812 B
Saddle Seat
Height of Back, 19¼ in.
Width of Seat, 16½ in.

C 635 B
Saddle Seat
Height of Back, 21 in.
Width of Seat, 16 in.

C 1815 D
Saddle Seat
Height of Back, 26 in.
Width between Arms, 16½ in.

C 400 D
Saddle Seat
Height of Back, 22 in.
Width between Arms, 17½ in.

C 845 A
Height of Back, 17½ in.
Width of Seat, 16 in.

C 918 A
Saddle Seat
Legs Cross-Rodded
Bent Braces from Legs to Seat
Height of Back, 20 in.
Width of Seat, 17 in.

C 635 A
Saddle Seat
Height of Back, 17½ in.
Width of Seat, 16 in.

C 541 A
Saddle Seat
Height of Back, 18½ in.
Width of Seat, 17½ in.

C 420 A
Rodded all around base under lower
Stretchers. Rodded from seat to top
Stretchers. Two rods through seat to
prevent splitting. Arms bolted to seat.
Height of Back, 17½ in.
Width of Seat, 17½ in.

For Finishes See Price List

C 1546 C
Open Cane Seat
Hoop Bolted to Legs
Height of Back, 14½ in.
Width of Seat, 19 in.

C 1546 CV
Veneer Seat
Hoop Bolted to Legs
Height of Back, 14½ in.
Width of Seat, 19 in.

C 459 AV
Veneer Seat
Height of Back, 17½ in.
Width of Seat, 16 in.

C 1160-22
Open Cane Seat
Height of Back, 10 in.
Width of Seat, 14½ in.
Height of Seat, 22 in.

C 466 A
Open Cane Seat
Height of Back, 17½ in.
Width of Seat, 16 in.
Special Steel Brace joins seat to rear leg.

C 466 AV
Veneer Seat
Height of Back, 17½ in.
Width of Seat, 16 in.
Special Steel Brace joins seat to rear leg.

C 462 AV
Veneer Seat
Height of Back, 18 in.
Width of Seat, 14½ in.
Special Steel Brace joins seat to rear leg.

C 453 A
Open or Woven Cane Seat
Height of Back, 18 in.
Width of Seat, 16 in.

C 453 AV
Veneer Seat
Height of Back, 18 in.
Width of Seat, 16 in.

For Finishes See Price List

C 1298 A
Slip Seat
Height of Back, 20½ in.
Width of Seat, 17 in.

C 1298 C
Slip Seat
Height of Back, 22 in.
Width between Arms, 18 in.

C 191 A
Leather Seat
Height of Back, 19 in.
Width of Seat, 16¾ in.

C 1285 A
Saddle Seat
Bolt Construction
Height of Back, 18 in.
Width of Seat, 17½ in.

C 2021 A
Saddle Seat
Height of Back, 18½ in.
Width of Seat, 16½ in.

C 889 A
Saddle Seat
Height of Back, 18 in.
Width of Seat, 18 in.

C 865 A
Saddle Seat
Height of Back, 18 in.
Width of Seat, 16½ in.

C 2010 A
Saddle Seat
Height of Back, 18¼ in.
Width of Seat, 17¾ in.

C 635 A
Saddle Seat
Height of Back, 17½ in.
Width of Seat, 16 in.

C 155 A
Saddle Seat
Height of Back, 18¾ in.
Width of Seat, 17 in.

For Finishes See Price List

C 3004 CX
Leather Box Cushion
Upholstered Back
Height of Back,   16   in.
Width between Arms, 20½ in.

C 3004 C XY X
Leather Box Cushion
Upholstered Back
Height of Back,   16   in.
Width between Arms, 20½ in.

C 3004 C
Leather Box Cushion
Height of Back,   16   in.
Width between Arms, 20½ in.

C 3004 C XY
Leather Box Cushion
Height of Back,   16   in.
Width between Arms, 20½ in.

C 3006 A
Saddle Seat
Height of Back, 18 in.
Width of Seat,   17 in.

C 3006 A XY
Saddle Seat
Height of Back, 18 in.
Width of Seat,   17 in.

C 3006 C
Saddle Seat
Height of Back,   20 in.
Width between Arms, 20 in.

C 3006 C XY
Saddle Seat
Height of Back,   20 in.
Width between Arms, 20 in.

For Finishes See Price List

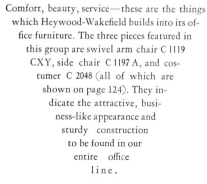

Comfort, beauty, service—these are the things which Heywood-Wakefield builds into its office furniture. The three pieces featured in this group are swivel arm chair C 1119 CXY, side chair C 1197 A, and costumer C 2048 (all of which are shown on page 124). They indicate the attractive, business-like appearance and sturdy construction to be found in our entire office line.

Comfort plus service

C 1444 CX
Saddle Seat
Leather Back
Height of Back,   16½ in.
Width between Arms,   19   in.

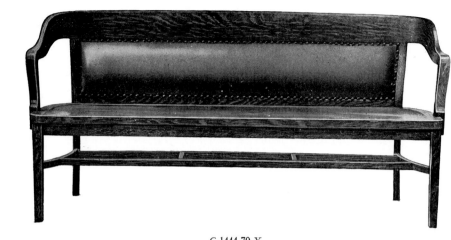

C 1444-70 X
Saddle Seat
Leather Back
Height of Back,   17½ in.
Width between Arms,   70   in.
Width Over All,   74   in.
OAK DL °°   **C 1444-46 X**   SOL. WAL. DU °°
Same as above, but shorter
Width between Arms,   46 in.
Width Over All,   49 in.

C 1444 C XY X
Saddle Seat
Leather Back
Height of Back,   16½ in.
Width between Arms,   19   in.

C 1456 C
Leather Box Cushion
Height of Back,   16   in.
Width between Arms,   19½ in.

C 1456 C XY
Leather Box Cushion
Height of Back,   16   in.
Width between Arms,   19½ in.

C 1456 CX
Leather Box Cushion
Upholstered Back
Height of Back,   16   in.
Width between Arms,   19½ in.

C 1456 C XY X
Leather Box Cushion
Upholstered Back
Height of Back,   16   in.
Width between Arms,   19½ in.

For Finishes See Price List

C 1444 C
Saddle Seat
Height of Back,   16½ in.
Width between Arms, 19 in.

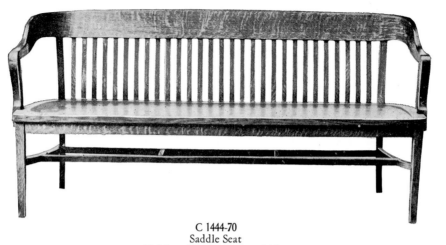

C 1444-70
Saddle Seat
Height of Back,   17½ in.
Width between Arms, 70 in.
Width Over All,   74 in.

C 1444 C XY
Saddle Seat
Height of Back,   16½ in.
Width between Arms, 19 in.

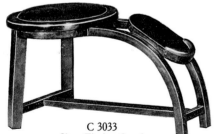

C 3033
Shoe Fitting Stool
Upholstered Seat and Footrest
Height of Seat,   14 in.
Width of Seat,   14 in.
Over All Length,   26 in.

C 1444 C XY PL
Perforated Leather Seat
Height of Back,   16½ in.
Width between Arms, 19 in.

C 3002 C
Saddle Seat
Height of Back,   17 in.
Width between Arms, 21 in.

C 3002 C XY
Saddle Seat
Height of Back,   17 in.
Width between Arms, 21 in.

For Finishes See Price List

C 2089 CXY
Saddle Seat
Height of Back,   23½ in.
Width between Arms, 18½ in.

C 2090 C
Saddle Seat
Height of Back,   23½ in.
Width between Arms, 18¾ in.

C 2065 C XY
Spring Filled Seat Cushion
Height of Back,   18 in.
Width between Arms,   19 in.

This chair has bolt construction.

C 3003 A
Saddle Seat
Height of Back, 17 in.
Width of Seat,   17 in.

C 3003 A XY
Saddle Seat
Height of Back, 17 in.
Width of Seat,   17 in.

C 3003 C
Saddle Seat
Height of Back,   19 in.
Width between Arms, 20 in.

C 3003 C XY
Saddle Seat
Height of Back,   19 in.
Width between Arms, 20 in.

The four chairs above have bolt construction.

For Finishes See Price List

C 1119 C
Saddle Seat
Height of Back,   15½ in.
Width between Arms, 19 in.

C 1119 C XY
Saddle Seat
Height of Back,   15½ in.
Width between Arms, 19 in.

C 1197 A
Saddle Seat
Height of Back, 17½ in.
Width of Seat, 17½ in.

C 1197 A XY
Saddle Seat
Height of Back, 17½ in.
Width of Seat, 17½ in.

C 1444-46
Width between Arms, 46 in.
Width over all,   49 in.

C 823
Hat Tree
Height, 72 in.
Base,   21 in.

C 2048
Hat Tree
Height, 72 in.
Base,   22 in.

C 2083
Hat Tree
Height, 65 in.
Base,   20 in.

For Finishes See Price List

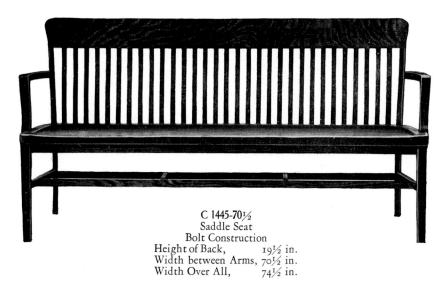

C 1445 A
Saddle Seat
Bolt Construction
Height of Back, 17 in.
Width of Seat, 17 in.

C 1445-70½
Saddle Seat
Bolt Construction
Height of Back, 19½ in.
Width between Arms, 70½ in.
Width Over All, 74½ in.

C 1445-47
Same as above, but shorter
Width between Arms, 47 in.
Width Over All, 50½ in.

C 1445 A XY
Saddle Seat
Bolt Construction
Height of Back, 17 in.
Width of Seat, 17 in.

C 1445 C
Saddle Seat
Bolt Construction
Height of Back, 19½ in.
Width between Arms, 19½ in.

C 1445 C XY
Saddle Seat
Bolt Construction
Height of Back, 19½ in.
Width between Arms, 19½ in.

C 1445 C XY PL
Perforated Leather Seat
Bolt Construction
Height of Back, 19½ in.
Width between Arms, 19½ in.

C 1445 AY
Saddle Seat
Bolt Construction
Height of Back, 17 in.
Width of Seat, 17 in.
Height of Seat, 30 in.

For Finishes See Price List

C 1113 A
Saddle Seat
Bolt Construction
Height of Back, 17 in.
Width of Seat, 17 in.

C 1113-48
Saddle Seat
Bolt Construction
Height of Back,   19   in.
Width between Arms, 48   in.
Width Over All,   50½ in.

C 1113 A XY
Saddle Seat
Bolt Construction
Height of Back, 17 in.
Width of Seat, 17 in.

C 1113 C
Saddle Seat
Bolt Construction
Height of Back,   19 in.
Width between Arms, 19 in.

C 1113 C XY
Saddle Seat
Bolt Construction
Height of Back,   19 in.
Width between Arms, 19 in.

For Finishes See Price List

C 1113 AY
Saddle Seat
Bolt Construction
Height of Back, 17 in.
Width of Seat, 17 in.
Height of Seat, 30 in.

C 1282 A
Saddle Seat
Bolt Construction
Height of Back, 17½ in.
Width of Seat, 18 in.

C 1282 A XY
Saddle Seat
Bolt Construction
Height of Back, 17½ in.
Width of Seat, 18 in.

C 1282 C
Saddle Seat
Bolt Construction
Height of Back,   18½ in.
Width between Arms, 19   in.

C 1282 C XY
Saddle Seat
Bolt Construction
Height of Back,   18½ in.
Width between Arms, 19   in.

C 1312 A
Saddle Seat
Bolt Construction
Height of Back, 17 in.
Width of Seat, 17½ in.

C 1312 A XY
Saddle Seat
Bolt Construction
Height of Back, 17 in.
Width of Seat, 17½ in.

C 1312 C
Saddle Seat
Bolt Construction
Height of Back,   18½ in.
Width between Arms, 19   in.

C 1312 C XY
Saddle Seat
Bolt Construction
Height of Back,   18½ in.
Width between Arms, 19   in.

For Finishes See Price List

C 918 A XY
Saddle Seat
Height of Back, 20 in.
Width of Seat, 17 in.

C 57 C
Saddle Seat
Height of Back,   22½ in.
Width between Arms, 18   in.

C 57 C XY
Saddle Seat
Height of Back,   22½ in.
Width between Arms, 18   in.

C 104 C XY
Woven Cane Seat and Back
Height of Back,   21 in.
Width between Arms, 18 in.

C 2076 C
Saddle Seat
Height of Back,   14½ in.
Width between Arms, 21½ in.
*Rodded Arm through Seat to Side
Stretcher and around Understock.
Two Rods through Seat.*

C 2075 C
Saddle Seat
Height of Back,   14½ in.
Width between Arms, 21½ in.
Rodded Arm through Seat to Side Stretcher

C 1121-46½
Saddle Seat
Height of Back,   24   in.
Width between Arms, 46½ in.
Width Over All,   54   in.

For Finishes See Price List

C 1150 AY
Saddle Seat
Leather Back
Height of Adjustable Back,
14½–18½ in.
Width of Seat, 15½ in.

C 1142 AY
Saddle Seat
Leather Back
Height of Adjustable Back,
11½–16 in.
Width of Seat, 15½ in.

C 1144 AY
Saddle Seat
Height of Adjustable Back,
13½–18½ in.
Width of Seat, 15½ in.

C 2082 AY
Seat and Back Upholstered in
Automobile Cloth
Height of Back, 13½ in.
Width of Seat, 16½ in.

C 51 A XY
Woven Cane Seat
Height of Back, 17 in.
Width of Seat, 16 in.

C 453 A XY
Woven Cane Seat
Height of Back, 17 in.
Width of Seat, 16 in.

C 1139 AY
Saddle Seat
Height of Adjustable Back,
11–15½ in.
Width of Seat, 15½ in.

C 1140 AY
Open Cane Seat and Back
Height of Adjustable Back,
11½–16 in.
Width of Seat, 15½ in.

For Finishes See Price List

C 795-30 Y X
Leather Seat
Diameter of Seat, 14½ in.
Height,   30   in.

C 795-30 Y
Open Cane Seat
Diameter of Seat, 14½ in.
Height,   30   in.

C 760-30 Y
Wood Seat
Diameter of Seat, 14 in.
Height,   30 in.

C 453 A Y
Open Cane Seat
Height of Back, 18 in.
Width of Seat, 16 in.
Height,   30 in.

C 51 A Y
Woven Cane Seat
Height of Back, 17 in.
Width of Seat, 16 in.
Height,   30 in.

C 1530-21 Y
Wood Seat
Diameter of Seat, 14 in.
Height,   21 in.

C 1530-33 Y
Wood Seat
Diameter of Seat, 14 in.
Height,   33 in.

C 5017-21 Y
Woven Cane Seat
Diameter of Seat, 14 in.
Height,   21 in.

C 5017-26 Y
Woven Cane Seat
Diameter of Seat, 14 in.
Height,   26 in.

C 5017-33 Y
Woven Cane Seat
Diameter of Seat, 14 in.
Height,   33 in.

For Finishes See Price List

C 380-30 R	**C 380-24 R**	**C 380-18R**	**C 5017-30**	**C 5017-25**	**C 5017-19**
Rodded	Rodded	Rodded	Woven Cane Seat	Woven Cane Seat	Woven Cane Seat
Diameter of Seat, 14 in.	Diameter of Seat, 13 in.	Diameter of Seat, 12 in.	Diameter of Seat, 14 in.	Diameter of Seat, 14 in.	Diameter of Seat, 14 in.
Height, 30 in.	Height, 24 in.	Height, 18 in.	Height, 30 in.	Height, 25 in.	Height, 19 in.

C 380-36	**C 380-30**	**C 380-24**	**C 380-18**
Diameter of Seat, 14 in.	Diameter of Seat, 14 in.	Diameter of Seat, 13 in.	Diameter of Seat, 12 in.
Height, 36 in.	Height, 30 in.	Height, 24 in.	Height, 18 in.

For Finishes See Price List

C 75-18
Wood Seat
Diameter of Seat, 12½ in.
Height,   18   in.

C 75-24
Wood Seat
Diameter of Seat, 12½ in.
Height,   24   in.

C 75-30
Wood Seat
Diameter of Seat, 12½ in.
Height,   30   in.

C 75-36
Wood Seat
Diameter of Seat, 13½ in.
Height,   36   in.

C 460-18
Rodded
Diameter of Seat, 12 in.
Height,   18 in.

C 460-24
Rodded
Diameter of Seat, 13 in.
Height,   24 in.

C 460-30
Rodded
Diameter of Seat, 14 in.
Height,   30 in.

C 5407-24
Height of Back, 17½ in.
Width of Seat, 16½ in.
Height of Seat, 24   in.

C 5407-30
Height of Back, 17½ in.
Width of Seat, 16½ in.
Height of Seat, 30   in.

For Finishes See Price List

C 1285 A
Saddle Seat
Bolt Construction
Height of Back, 18   in.
Width of Seat, 17½ in.

C 1285 TA
With Hat Rack
Saddle Seat
Bolt Construction
Height of Back, 18   in.
Width of Seat,   17½ in.

C 889 A
Saddle Seat
Height of Back,   18 in.
Width of Seat,   18 in.

C 889 TA
With Hat Rack
Saddle Seat
Bolt Construction
Height of Back, 18½ in.
Width of Seat,   18½ in.

C 1284 TA
With Hat Rack
Saddle Seat
Bolt Construction
Height of Back, 14½ in.
Width of Seat,   17½ in.

C 430 TA
Double Cane Seat
Height of Back, 18¼ in.
Width of Seat,   23 in.

C 430 STA
Same as above, but with
saddle seat. Both this
and the chair shown above
can be furnished with
left-hand shelf.

C 541 TA
Saddle Seat
Height of Back, 19½ in.
Width of Seat,   17 in.

C 2010 TA
Saddle Seat
Height of Back, 18¼ in.
Width of Seat,   17¾ in.

C 1293 TA
With Hat Rack
Saddle Seat
Bolt Construction
Height of Back, 19½ in.
Width of Seat,   17 in.

C 2075 TA
Saddle Seat
Height of Back,   14½ in.
Width between Arms, 21½ in.

For Finishes See Price List

C 20 A B&HR
Close Woven Cane Seat
With Hat Rack
Height of Back, 17 in.
Width of Seat, 16¾ in.

C 18 A B&HR
Woven Cane Seat
Book and Hat Rack
Height of Back, 20 in.
Width of Seat, 18½ in.

C 635 A B&HR
Saddle Seat
Book and Hat Rack
Height of Back, 17½ in.
Width of Seat, 15½ in.

C 889 A B&HR
Saddle Seat
Book and Hat Rack
Height of Back, 18 in.
Width of Seat, 18½ in.

C 889 A HR
Saddle Seat
Hat Rack
Height of Back, 18 in.
Width of Seat, 18½ in.

C 3001 A
Height of Back, 20 in.
Width of Seat, 17 in.

C 865 A
Saddle Seat
Height of Back, 18 in.
Width of Seat, 16½ in.

C 888 A
Saddle Seat
Height of Back, 18 in.
Width of Seat, 17 in.

C 1376
Saddle Seat
Height of Back, 22 in.
Width between Arms, 17 in.
Height of Seat, 25 in.
Width Over All, 23 in.

C 242
Saddle Seat
Height of Back, 21 in.
Width between Arms, 18 in.
Height of Seat, 25 in.
Width Over All, 27 in.

For Finishes See Price List

C 9 H
(As Table Chair)
Open Cane Seat and Back
Height of Back, 16 in.
Width between Arms, 11½ in.
Furnished with Enamel or Aluminum Tray Extra

C 9 H
(As Youth's Diner)
Open Cane Seat and Back
Height of Back, 16 in.
Width between Arms, 11½ in.
Furnished with Enamel or Aluminum Tray Extra

C 9 H
(As Carriage)
Open Cane Seat and Back
Height of Back, 16 in.
Width between Arms, 11½ in.
Furnished with Enamel or Aluminum Tray Extra

C 9 H
(As Rocker)
Open Cane Seat and Back
Height of Back, 16 in.
Width between Arms, 11½ in.
Furnished with Enamel or Aluminum Tray Extra

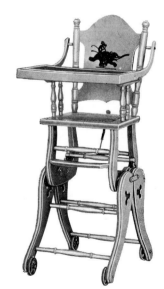

C 799 H
(As Table Chair)
Open Cane Seat and Back
Adjustable to four positions as shown
on C 9 H above
Height of Back, 18½ in.
Width between Arms, 11½ in.
Furnished with Enamel or Aluminum Tray Extra

C 891 H
(As Table Chair)
Open Cane Seat
Adjustable to four positions as shown
on C 9 H above
Height of Back, 17 in.
Width between Arms, 11½ in.
Furnished with Enamel or Aluminum Tray Extra

C 947 H
(As Table Chair)
Open Cane Seat
Adjustable to all the positions shown on
C 9 H above, except rocker
Height of Back, 17 in.
Width between Arms, 11¼ in.
Furnished with Enamel or Aluminum Tray Extra

C 2058 H
(As Table Chair)
Open Cane Seat
Adjustable to four positions as shown on
C 9 H above
Height of Back, 16½ in.
Width between Arms, 11 in.
Furnished with Enamel or Aluminum Tray Extra

For Finishes See Price List

C 3040 N
Saddle Seat
Height of Back, 17¾ in.
Width between Arms, 12¼ in.

C 3039 N
Saddle Seat
Height of Back, 17½ in.
Width between Arms, 11¼ in.

C 3035 N
Saddle Seat
Height of Back, 17 in.
Width between Arms, 11¼ in.

C 3038 N
Saddle Seat
Height of Back, 17 in.
Width between Arms, 11½ in.

C 3034 N
Saddle Seat
Height of Back, 18 in.
Width between Arms, 11¼ in.

C 3040 H
Saddle Seat
Height of Back, 17¾ in.
Width between Arms, 12¼ in.
*Furnished with Enamel or Aluminum
Tray Extra*

C 3039 H
Saddle Seat
Height of Back, 17½ in.
Width between Arms, 11¼ in.
*Furnished with Enamel or Aluminum
Tray Extra*

C 3035 H
Saddle Seat
Height of Back, 17 in.
Width between Arms, 11¼ in.
*Furnished with Enamel or Aluminum
Tray Extra*

C 3038 H
Saddle Seat
Height of Back, 17 in.
Width between Arms, 11½ in.
*Furnished with Enamel or Aluminum
Tray Extra*

C 3034 H
Saddle Seat
Height of Back, 18 in.
Width between Arms, 11¼ in.
*Furnished with Enamel or Aluminum
Tray Extra*

For Finishes See Price List

C 3036 N Saddle Seat Height of Back, 17 in. Width between Arms, 12¼ in.	**C 3037 K** Saddle Seat Height of Back, 17 in. Width between Arms, 12¼ in.	**C 1826 N** Height of Back, 16¾ in. Width between Arms, 11 in.	**C 1825 N** Height of Back, 16¾ in. Width between Arms, 11 in.	**C 1824 N** Height of Back, 16¾ in. Width between Arms, 11 in.

C 3036 H Saddle Seat Height of Back, 17 in. Width between Arms, 12¼ in. *Furnished with Enamel or Aluminum Tray Extra*	**C 3037 H** Saddle Seat Height of Back, 17 in. Width between Arms, 12¼ in.	**C 1826 H** Height of Back, 16¾ in. Width between Arms, 11 in. *Furnished with Enamel or Aluminum Tray Extra*	**C 1825 H** Height of Back, 16¾ in. Width between Arms, 11 in. *Furnished with Enamel or Aluminum Tray Extra*	**C 1824 H** Height of Back, 16¾ in. Width between Arms, 11 in. *Furnished with Enamel or Aluminum Tray Extra*

For Finishes See Price List

C 1821 N
Height of Back,   16¾ in.
Width between Arms, 11½ in.

C 1822 N
Height of Back,   16¼ in.
Width between Arms, 11½ in.

C 1820 N
Height of Back,   16 in.
Width between Arms, 11½ in.

C 71 N
Height of Back,   16 in.
Width between Arms, 11½ in.

C 3041 H
Saddle Seat
Height of Back, 17 in.
Width of Seat, 14 in.

C 1821 H
Height of Back,   16¾ in.
Width between Arms, 11½ in.
*Furnished with Enamel or Aluminum
Tray Extra*

C 1822 H
Height of Back,   16¼ in.
Width between Arms, 11½ in.
*Furnished with Enamel or Aluminum
Tray Extra*

C 1820 H
Height of Back,   16 in.
Width between Arms, 11½ in.
*Furnished with Enamel or Aluminum
Tray Extra*

C 71 H
Height of Back,   16 in.
Width between Arms, 11½ in.

C 2031 H
Height of Back,   17 in.
Width between Arms, 12½ in.

For Finishes See Price List

C 1829 H
Height of Back, 16¾ in.
Width between Arms, 11 in.
*Furnished with Enamel or Aluminum
Tray Extra*

C 1153 H
Height of Back, 16½ in.
Width of Seat, 15 in.
Height of Seat, 22 in.

C 1823
Height of Back,   16 in.
Width between Arms, 11½ in.

C 1828
Height of Back,   16 in.
Width between Arms, 11 in.

C 1827
Height of Back,   16¾ in.
Width between Arms, 11 in.

C 1343
Height of Back,   15½ in.
Width between Arms, 11 in.

C 2021 K-14
Saddle Seat

Height of Back, 16 in.
Width of Seat, 14½ in.
Height of Seat, 14 in.

C 2021 K-12
Saddle Seat

Height of Back, 13¼ in.
Width of Seat, 12¼ in.
Height of Seat, 12 in.

C 2021 K-10
Saddle Seat

Height of Back, 13¼ in.
Width of Seat, 12¼ in.
Height of Seat, 10 in.

For Finishes See Price List

C 5721 K-10 Height of Back, 12 in. Width of Seat, 12 in. Height of Seat, 10 in.	**C 5721 K-12** Height of Back, 14½ in. Width of Seat, 13½ in. Height of Seat, 12 in.	**C 5721 K-14** Height of Back, 15 in. Width of Seat, 13½ in. Height of Seat, 14 in.	**C 516 K-10** Height of Back, 12½ in. Width of Seat, 11½ in. Height of Seat, 10 in.	**C 516 K-12** Height of Back, 14 in. Width of Seat, 12½ in. Height of Seat, 12 in.	**C 516 K-14** Height of Back, 15 in. Width of Seat, 14½ in. Height of Seat, 14 in.

C 2077 K-10 Scoop Seat Height of Back, 11¾ in. Width of Seat, 11¾ in. Height of Seat, 10 in.	**C 2077 K-12** Scoop Seat Height of Back, 11¾ in. Width of Seat, 11¾ in. Height of Seat, 12 in.	**C 2077 K-14** Scoop Seat Height of Back, 11¾ in. Width of Seat, 11¾ in. Height of Seat, 14 in.	**C 218 K-10** Height of Back, 10 in. Width of Seat, 13 in. Height of Seat, 10 in.	**C 218 K-12** Height of Back, 10 in. Width of Seat, 13 in. Height of Seat, 12 in.	**C 218 K-14** Height of Back, 12 in. Width of Seat, 14 in. Height of Seat, 14 in.

For Finishes See Price List

C 1281-42
Woven Fibre Seat
Height of Back,   22½ in.
Width between Arms, 42 in.
Width Over All,   47 in.

C 1281 D
Woven Fibre Seat
Height of Back,   21½ in.
Width between Arms, 19½ in.

C 1281 C
Woven Fibre Seat
Height of Back,   22 in.
Width between Arms, 19½ in.

C 1281 A
Woven Fibre Seat
Height of Back, 19½ in.
Width of Seat,   17½ in.

C 2001 G
Diameter,   36 in.
Height,   30 in.

C 2070 D
Double Cane Seat
Height of Back,   28 in.
Width between Arms, 19 in.

C 2070 C
Double Cane Seat
Height of Back,   22½ in.
Width between Arms, 19 in.

C 1283 A
Double Cane Seat
Height of Back, 18 in.
Width of Seat,   17½ in.

For Finishes See Price List

C 2055 C
Double Cane Seat
Height of Back,   21¾ in.
Width between Arms, 19   in.

C 2055 D
Double Cane Seat
Height of Back,   21¾ in.
Width between Arms, 19   in.

C 136 D
Double Cane Seat and Back
Height of Back,   30 in.
Width between Arms, 20½ in.

C 135 D
Double Cane Seat and Back
Height of Back,   30½ in.
Width between Arms, 19½ in.

C 133 D
Double Cane Seat and Back
Height of Back,   24 in.
Width between Arms, 18 in.

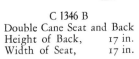

C 1346 B
Double Cane Seat and Back
Height of Back,   17 in.
Width of Seat,   17 in.

C 134-37
Double Cane Seat and Back
Height of Back,   21½ in.
Width between Arms, 37   in.
Width Over All,   45   in.

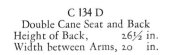

C 134 D
Double Cane Seat and Back
Height of Back,   26½ in.
Width between Arms, 20 in.

C 134 C
Double Cane Seat and Back
Height of Back,   21½ in.
Width between Arms, 20 in.

For Finishes See Price List

142

142

C 2056 D
Double Cane Seat
Height of Back,   27½ in.
Width between Arms, 18½ in.

C 2069 C
Double Cane Seat
Height of Back,   19½ in.
Width between Arms, 19   in.

C 2069 D
Double Cane Seat
Height of Back,   22½ in.
Width between Arms, 19   in.

C 127 C
Double Cane Seat
Height of Back,   17½ in.
Width between Arms, 19½ in.

C 127 D
Double Cane Seat
Height of Back,   21 in.
Width between Arms, 19½ in.

C 174 D
Double Cane Seat
Height of Back,   27 in.
Width between Arms, 19½ in.

C 649 D
Double Cane Seat
Height of Back,   30½ in.
Width between Arms, 20½ in.

C 964 A
Double Cane Seat
Height of Back, 18½ in.
Width of Seat, 17½ in.

C 964 B
Double Cane Seat
Height of Back, 18½ in.
Width of Seat, 17½ in.

C 126 N
Child's Rocker
Double Cane Seat
Height of Back,   16½ in.
Width between Arms, 14½ in.

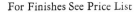
For Finishes See Price List

C 747
Woven Cane Top
72 x 25 in.

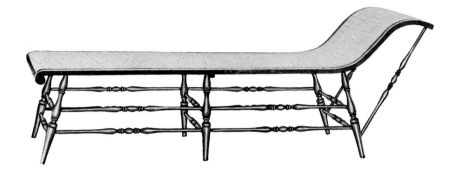

C 2040
Woven Cane Top
73 x 25¼ in.

C 170
Woven Cane Top
72 x 25 in.

C 710
Woven Cane Top
72 x 25 in.

For Finishes See Price List

C 2071
Reclining Back and Leg Rest
Open Cane Seat and Back
Steel Wheels   Cushion Tires

Height of Back,	31¼ in.
Height of Seat,	19½ in.
Length of Foot Rest,	16 in.
Width between Arms,	19¼ in.
Depth of Seat,	20 in.
Diameter of Large Wheels,	26 in.
Diameter of Small Wheels,	10 in.
Width over all,	29¼ in.

Push Handle Extra

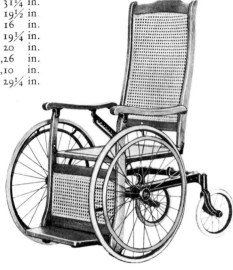

C 2072
Reclining Back and Leg Rest
Open Cane Seat and Back
Steel Wheels   Cushion Tires

Height of Back,	31¼ in.
Height of Seat,	19½ in.
Length of Foot Rest,	16 in.
Width between Arms,	17 in.
Depth of Seat,	20 in.
Diameter of Large Wheels,	26 in.
Diameter of Small Wheels,	10 in.
Width over all,	25¾ in.

Push Handle Extra

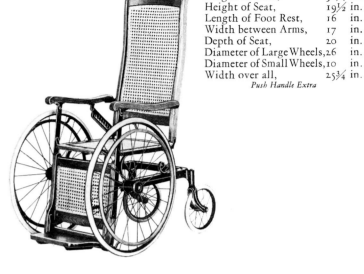

C 2073
Reclining Back and Adjustable
Leg Rests
(Back Reclines Separately)
Open Cane Seat and Back
Steel Wheels   Cushion Tires

Height of Back,	31¼ in.
Height of Seat,	19½ in.
Length of Foot Rests,	16 in.
Width between Arms,	19 in.
Depth of Seat,	20 in.
Diameter of Large Wheels,	26 in.
Diameter of Small Wheels,	10 in.
Width over all,	29¼ in.

Push Handle Extra

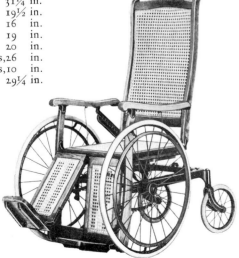

C 960
Cabinet Chair

Height of Back,	25½ in.
Width between Arms,	18½ in.

C 2074
Reclining Back and Adjustable
Leg Rests
(Back Reclines Separately)
Open Cane Seat and Back
Steel Wheels   Cushion Tires

Height of Back,	31¼ in.
Height of Seat,	19½ in.
Length of Foot Rests,	16 in.
Width between Arms,	17 in.
Depth of Seat,	20 in.
Diameter of Large Wheels,	26 in.
Diameter of Small Wheels,	10 in.
Width over all,	25¾ in.

Push Handle Extra

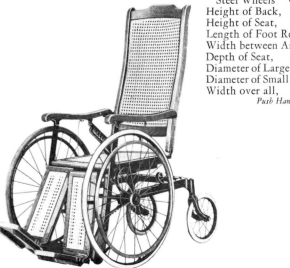

For Finishes See Price List

C 186
Slat Seat and Back
Height of Back,   29½ in.
Width between Arms, 19¼ in.

C 185
Open Cane Seat and Back
Height of Back,   30   in.
Width between Arms, 21¼ in.

C 184
Slat Seat and Back
Height of Back,   30   in.
Width between Arms, 21¼ in.

C 183
Open Cane Seat and Back
Height of Back,   27½ in.
Width between Arms, 18½ in.

C 182
Slat Seat and Back
Height of Back,   29¾ in.
Width between Arms, 19¾ in.

C 180
Canvas Reclining Chair
Height of Back,   28½ in.
Width between Arms, 18¼ in.

For Finishes See Price List

C 181
Slat Seat and Back
Height of Back,   23½ in.
Width between Arms, 20¾ in.

C 5804
Slat Seat
Height of Back, 20   in.
Width of Seat,   14¼ in.

C 1501
Veneer Seat and Back
Height of Back, 18 in.
Width of Seat, 15 in.

C 5796
Slat Seat and Back
Height of Back, 17 in.
Width of Seat,   14 in.

C 5795
Slat Seat
Height of Back, 18½ in.
Width of Seat, 15½ in.

C 1228
Slat Seat
Height of Back, 18 in.
Width of Seat,   14 in.

C 1235
Slat Seat
In Sections, or Single
Height of Back, 18½ in.
Width of Seat,   14   in.

C 1602
Slat Seat
Height of Back, 17½ in.
Width of Seat,   14   in.

C 5798
Slat Seat
Chair folds absolutely flat
Height of Back, 15¾ in.
Width of Seat,   14   in.

C 5809
Upholstered Seat
Height of Back,   16 in.
Width of Seat,   13 in.

For Finishes See Price List

C 223
Canvas or Carpet Seat
Seat,   14 x 14 in.
Height,   19 in.

C 222
Canvas or Carpet Seat
Height of Back, 16 in.
Width of Seat, 13½ in.

OC 296
Steel Folding Chair
Slat Seat
Height of Back,   16 in.
Width of Seat,   14 in.

OC 267
Steel Folding Chair
Slat Seat
Height of Back, 16 in.
Width of Seat, 17½ in.

C 1345
Imitation Leather Slip Seat
Chair folds absolutely flat
Height of Back, 17¼ in.
Width of Seat,   14 in.

T 230
A strong, comfortable chair with inserted panels of cane webbing on seat and back.

T 285
A sturdy, slat back and seat portable chair that will withstand the most severe use.

T 274
A strong, yet light, portable chair of full cabinet frame construction with a comfortable, curved back.

T 241
The graceful shape of the back lends a distinctive appearance to this portable veneer chair.

The four styles shown above are from our portable chair line. A complete catalogue and price list will be sent on request. Simply write to the nearest Heywood-Wakefield warehouse for your copy.

For Finishes See Price List

Reeds, Chair Cane, and Cane Webbing

THOUSANDS of repair departments in furniture stores are using Heywood-Wakefield Reed and Cane. They do so because they realize the advantages in buying Reed and Cane from a Company that manufactures every kind necessary for use in America.

Our own agents in the Far East inspect and buy all of the rattan shipped to our factories. You are thus assured of securing reeds, chair cane, and cane webbing of dependable quality.

The reeds which we manufacture will run from 1-32 inch to 3-4 inch in diameter and the stock is sold by weight. All reeds are of first quality. We also manufacture several sizes of Reed Spline in lengths from 8 to 14 feet.

Chair Cane is made in widths known as Carriage, Superfine, Fine Fine, Fine, Narrow Medium, Medium, and Common. The grades are Long Selected, Extra No. 1, and No. 1. The Fine, Narrow Medium, Medium, and Common widths are also furnished in a No. 2 grade.

The strands are measured and put up in bunches of 1,000 feet. Full bales contain 100M feet.

Open Cane Webbing is manufactured from Superfine, Fine Fine, Fine, Narrow Medium, Medium, and Common Cane. The Superfine is manufactured in Extra No. 1 grade only; the Fine Fine in Extra No. 1 and No. 1; the Fine, Narrow Medium, Medium, and Common in Extra No. 1, No. 1, and No. 2. Open Cane Webbing is produced in rolls in widths ranging from about 8 inches to 25 inches. It is sold by the lineal foot.

Close Woven Cane Webbing is manufactured from Fine Fine, Fine, Narrow Medium, Medium, and Common Cane. The Fine Fine is furnished in Extra No. 1 and No. 1 grades only. The Fine, Narrow Medium, Medium, and Common are furnished in Extra No. 1, No. 1, and No. 2 grades.

Orders for Open and Close Woven Cane Webbing are accepted only in multiples of 100 lineal feet.

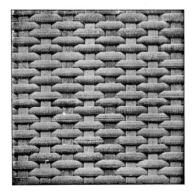

Fine Close Woven Cane Webbing

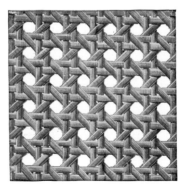

Superfine Open Cane Webbing

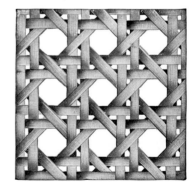

Medium Open Cane Webbing

The actual size illustrations above show in a small measure the variety of cane offered by Heywood-Wakefield.
Write for full information and price list on reeds, chair cane, and cane webbing.

INDEX

REED AND FIBRE FURNITURE

Pages 5-84 inclusive

INDEX

WOOD FURNITURE

Pages 86-149 inclusive

Price Guide

Page	Position	Value
7	TL	325
	TC	750
	TR	350
	BL	250
	BC1	250
	BC2	200
	BR	125
8	TL	350
	TC	675
	TR	350
	BL	125
	BC1	150
	BC2	150
	BR	350
9	TL	250
	TC	450
	TR	250
	BL	250
	BC	500
	BR	250
11	TL	250
	TC	500
	TR	250
	BL	250
	BC	250
	BR	250
12	TL	250
	TC	500
	TR	250
	BL	250
	BC	500

Page	Position	Value
	BR	250
13	TL	250
	TR	500
	BL	300
	BC	550
	BR	300
15	TL	250
	TC1	250
	TC2	250
	TR	250
	BL	150
	BC	500 set
	BR	300
16	TL	250
	TC	450
	TR	250
	BL	225
	BC	400
	BR	225
17	TL	225
	TC	400
	TR	225
	BL	200
	BC	350
	BR	200
19	TL	200
	TC	350
	TR	200
	BL	150
	BC1	150
	BC2	250
	BR	225
20	TL	200

Page	Position	Value
	TC	400
	TR	200
	BL	200
	BC	350
	BR	200
21	TL	150
	TC	350
	TR	150
	BL	200
	BC	150
	BR	200
23	TL	375
	TC	650
	TR	375
	BL	375
	BC	650
	BR	375
24	TL	400
	TC	700
	TR	400
	BL	300
	BC	800
	BR	225
25	TL	175
	TC1	175
	TC2	550
	TR	200
	BL	400
	BC	700
	BR	400
26	TL	375
	TC	650
	TR	375

Page	Position	Value
	BL	350
	BC1	325
	BC2	350
	BR	225
27	TL	400
	TC	700
	TR	400
	BL	400
	BC	650
	BR	400
28	TL	375
	TC	650
	TR	375
	BL	375
	BC	650
	BR	375
29	TL	425
	TC	850
	TR	425
	BL	375
	BC	650
	BR	375
30	TL	400
	TC	650
	TR	400
	BL	250
	BC	450
	BR	200
31	TL	375
	TC	650
	TR	375
	BL	350
	BC	600

Page	Position	Value	Page	Position	Value	Page	Position	Value	Page	Position	Value
	BR	350	40	TL	325	48	TL	325		TC2	125
33	TL	300		TC	600		TC	600		TR	150
	TC	550		TR	325		TR	325		BL	175
	TR	300		BL	600		BL	300		BC1	175
	BL	200		BR	700		BC	550		BC2	200
	BC	150	41	TL	300		BR	300		BR	150
	BR	250		TC	350	49	TL	325	55	TL	650
34	TL	350		TR	575		TC	600		TR	525
	TC	600		BL	350		TR	325		C	425
	TR	350		BC	650		BL	325		BL	650
	BL	350		BR	350		BC	800		BR	575
	BC	200	43	TL	325		BR	350	56	TL	150
	BR	350		TC	600	50	TL	325		TC1	175
35	TL	325		TR	325		TC	600		TC2	150
	TC	600		BL	325		TR	325		TR	175
	TR	325		BC	600		BL	325		BL	150
	BL	250		BR	325		BC	250		BC1	150
	BC	800	44	TL	325		BR	325		BC2	150
	BR	200		TC	600	51	TL	325		BR	175
36	TL	300		TR	325		TC	600	57	TL	175
	TC	550		BL	325		TR	325		TC1	150
	TR	300		BC	800		BL	300		TC2	150
	BL	125		BR	325		BC	550		TR	150
	BC	325	45	TL	950		BR	300		BL	150
	BR	150		TR	325	52	TL	300		BC1	150
37	TL	200		BL	325		TC	450		BC2	150
	TC1	150		BC	600		TR	300		BR	150
	TC2	175		BR	325		BL	300	58	All	20 each
	TR	175	46	TL	350		BC	450	59	TL	325
	BL	200		TC	650		BR	300		TC	300
	BC	200		TR	350	53	TL	325		TR	350
	BR	200		BL	350		TC1	325		BL	325
39	TL	325		BC	800		TC2	350		BR	325
	TC	600		BR	250		TR	350	60	TL	300
	TR	325	47	TL	325		BL	350		TC	300
	BL	350		TC	600		BC1	350		TR	275
	BC	650		TR	325		BC2	350		BL	200
	BR	350		BL	200		BR	350		BC1	250
				BC	225	54	TL	250		BC2	250
				BR	175		TC1	125		BR	250

Page	Position	Value
61	TL	350
	TC	250
	TR	200
	BL	250
	BC	325
	BR	225
62	TL	200
	TC	200
	TR	250
	BL	125
	BC1	125
	BC2	150
	BR	200
63	TL	200
	TC1	200
	TC2	300
	TR	200
	BL	275
	BC1	150
	BC2	250
	BR	250
64	TL	150
	TC1	150
	TC2	250
	TR	200
	BL	225
	BC1	250
	BC2	200
	BR	200
65	TL	200
	TC1	200
	TC2	150
	TR	200
	BL	150
	BC1	150
	BC2	150
	BR	200
66	TL	175
	TC1	175
	TC2	175
	TR	350
	BL	400
	BC	1250
	BR	1050
67	TL	575
	TC	575
	TR	575
	BL	725 set
	BC	550
	BR	700
68	TL	550
	TC	500
	TR	275
	BL	325
	BC1	575
	BC2	475
	BR	225
69	TL	550
	TC	225
	TR	200
	BL	225
	BC	225
	BR	200
70	TL	225
	TC	225
	TR	200
	BL	200
	BC1	200
	BC2	200
	BR	200
71	TL	250
	TC1	325
	TC2	175
	TC3	125
	TC4	125
	TR	150
	BL	75
	BC1	75
	BC2	525
	BC3	95
	BR	95
72	TL	250
	TC1	125
	TC2	175
	TC3	175
	TR	200
	BL	150
	BC1	250
	BC2	325
	BC3	325
	BR	250
73	TL	350
	TC1	350
	TC2	350
	TC3	325
	TR	325
	BL	250
	BR	200,225, 250
74	TL	625
	TC	625
	TR	425
	BL	125
	BC1	125
	BC2	150
	BC3	200
	BR	375
75	T	175 each
	B	200 each
76	TL	425
	TR	375
	BL	425
	BR	625
77	BL	325
	BC	600
	BR	325
78	TL	325
	TC	600
	TR	325
	BL	325
	BC	600
	BR	325
79	TL	325
	TC	600
	TR	325
	BL	525
	BR	800
80	TL	325
	TC	600
	TR	325
	BL	325
	BC	625
	BR	325
81	TL	325
	TC	600
	TR	325
	BL	325
	BC	450
	BR	325
82	TL	375
	TC	650
	TR	375
	BL	375
	BC	650
	BR	375
83	TL	375
	TC	525
	TR	375
	BL	350
	BC	525
	BR	350
84	TL	200
	TC1	200
	TC2	250
	TR	200
	BL	200
	BC1	250
	BC2	250

Page	Position	Value
	BR	150
87	TL	50
	TC	120
	TR	60
	BL	60
	BC	150
	BR	75
88	T	60 each
	BL	60
	BC1	50
	BC2	50
	BC3	50
89	TL	50
	TC1	50
	TC2	50
	TR	75
	B	90 each
90	TL	50
	TC1	85
	TC2	65
	TR	75
	BL	50
	BC1	125
	BC2	125
	BR	75
91	TL	60
	TC1	45
	TC2	45
	TR	90
	BL	60
	BC1	35 each
	BC2	120
	BR	90
92	L	175
	T	400
	R	200
	B	500
93	L	225
	T	500
	R	250
	B	600
94	L	125
	T	550
	R	200
	B	150
95	TL	75
	TC	110
	TR	175
	BL	350
	BR	225
96	TL	50
	TC	125
	TR	60
	BL	50
	BC1	50
	BC2	50
	BR	40
97	TL	50
	TC1	50
	TC2	50
	TC3	40
	TR	40
	BL	40
	BC1	40
	BC2	40
	BC3	60
	BR	60
98	TL	60
	TC1	60
	TC2	60
	TR	75
	BL	60
	BC1	75
	BC2	60
	BR	75
99	TL	60
	TC1	60
	TC2	60
	TR	70
	BL	60
	BC1	60
	BC2	75
	BR	50
100	All	300
101	TL	50
	TC1	60
	TC2	50
	TC3	50
	TR	50
	BL	60
	BC1	60
	BC2	75
	BC3	50
	BR	50
102	T	50 each
	B	50 each
103	T	50 each
	BL	50
	BC1	40
	BC2	40
	BC3	40
	BR	40
105	L	125
	T	625
	R	110
	B	200
106	L	120
	T	140
	R	110
	B	65
107	TL	175
	TR	90
	BL	110
	BR	40
109	TL	40
	TC	150
	TR	150
	BL	40
	BC	95
	BR	95
110	TL	175
	TC	95
	TR	250
	BL	175
	BC	110
	BR	175
111	TL	95
	TR	95
	BL	95
	BC	95
	BR	95
113	TL	150
	TR	150
	BL	65
	BC	65
	BR	65
114	TL	40
	TC	55
	TR	75
	BL	75
	BC	75
	BR	95
115	T	40 each
	BL	40
	BC1	35
	BC2	20
	BR	20
116	TL	40
	TC1	50
	TC2	50
	TC3	65
	TR	60
	BL	40
	BC1	40
	BC2	40
	BC3	40
	BR	25
117	TL	95

Page	Position	Value
	TC1	95
	TC2	75
	TR	95
	B	75 each
118	TL	50
	TC1	50
	TC2	65
	TC3	65
	TR	65
	B	65 each
119	TL	75
	TC1	95
	TC2	75
	TR	95
	BL	25
	BC1	65
	BC2	35
	BR	75
121	TL	75
	TC	350
	TR	95
	BL	75
	BC1	95
	BC2	75
	BR	95
122	TL	65
	TC	350
	TR	95
	BL	40
	BC1	85
	BC2	65
	BR	95
123	TL	125
	TC	60
	TR	65
	BL	25
	BC1	65
	BC2	35
	BR	75
124	TL	65
	TC1	95
	TC2	35
	TR	65
	BL	225
	BC1	25
	BC2	25
	BR	25
125	TL	40
	TC	375
	TR	60
	BL	40
	BC1	65
	BC2	65
	BR	125
126	TL	40
	TC	275
	TR	60
	BL	40
	BC	65
	BR	125
127	TL	40
	TC1	60
	TC2	40
	TR	65
	BL	45
	BC1	60
	BC2	40
	BR	65
128	TL	75
	TC1	90
	TC2	125
	TR	110
	BL	40
	BC	40
	BR	350
129	TL	45
	TC1	45
	TC2	50
	TR	45
	BL	95
	BC1	95
	BC2	45
	BR	50
130	TL	65
	TC1	65
	TC2	65
	TC3	125
	TR	125
	BL	55
	BC1	65
	BC2	55
	BC3	65
	BR	75
131	TL	35
	TC1	30
	TC2	25
	TC3	35
	TC4	30
	TR	25
	BL	35
	BC1	35
	BC2	35
	BR	25
132	TL	25
	TC1	30
	TC2	35
	TR	45
	BL	25
	BC1	30
	BC2	35
	BC3	45
	BR	50
133	TL	40
	TC1	35
	TC2	40
	TC3	35
	TR	35
	BL	35
	BC1	35
	BC2	35
	BC3	35
	BR	25
134	TL	65
	TC1	60
	TC2	65
	TC3	65
	TR	65
	BL	65
	BC1	65
	BC2	65
	BC3	125
	BR	125
135	T	375 each
	BL	250
	BC1	275
	BC2	225
	BR	125
136	T	60 each
	B	95 each
137	TL	60
	TC1	40
	TC2	60
	TC3	60
	TR	60
	BL	95
	BC1	75
	BC2	95
	BC3	95
	BR	95
138	TL	60
	TC1	60
	TC2	60
	TC3	45
	TR	65
	B	95 each
139	TL	95
	TC1	40
	TC2	75

Page	Position	Value
	TR	75
	BL	70
	BC1	60
	BC2	40
	BC3	40
	BR	40
140	TL	30
	TC1	30
	TC2	30
	TC3	25
	TC4	25
	TR	25
	BL	30
	BC1	30
	BC2	30
	BC3	20
	BC4	20
	BR	20
141	TL	275
	TC1	95
	TC2	80
	TR	70
	BL	125
	BC1	95
	BC2	80
	BR	60
142	TL	85
	TC1	110
	TC2	95
	TR	95
	BL	95
	BC1	80
	BC2	250
	BC3	95
	BR	80
143	TL	75
	TC1	55
	TC2	75
	TC3	55
	TR	75
	BL	95
	BC1	95
	BC2	50
	BC3	75
	BR	75
144	TL	275
	TR	275
	BL	275
	BR	275
145	TL	195
	C	95
	TR	195
	BL	195
	BR	195
146	TL	75
	TC	95
	TR	75
	BL	95
	BC	75
	BR	65
147	TL	45
	TC1	20
	TC2	20
	TC3	20
	TR	20
	BL	20
	BC1	20
	BC2	15
	BC3	15
	BR	15
148	TL	15
	TC1	20
	TC2	20
	TC3	35
	TR	20
	BL	45
	BC1	25
	BC2	25
	BR	25

WAKEFIELD-MASSACHUSETTS

CHICAGO - ILLINOIS

GARDNER-MASSACHUSETTS

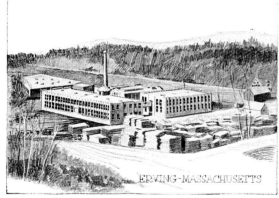

ERVING-MASSACHUSETTS

ORILLIA-CANADA

MENOMINEE-MICHIGAN

Heywood-Wakefield Factories

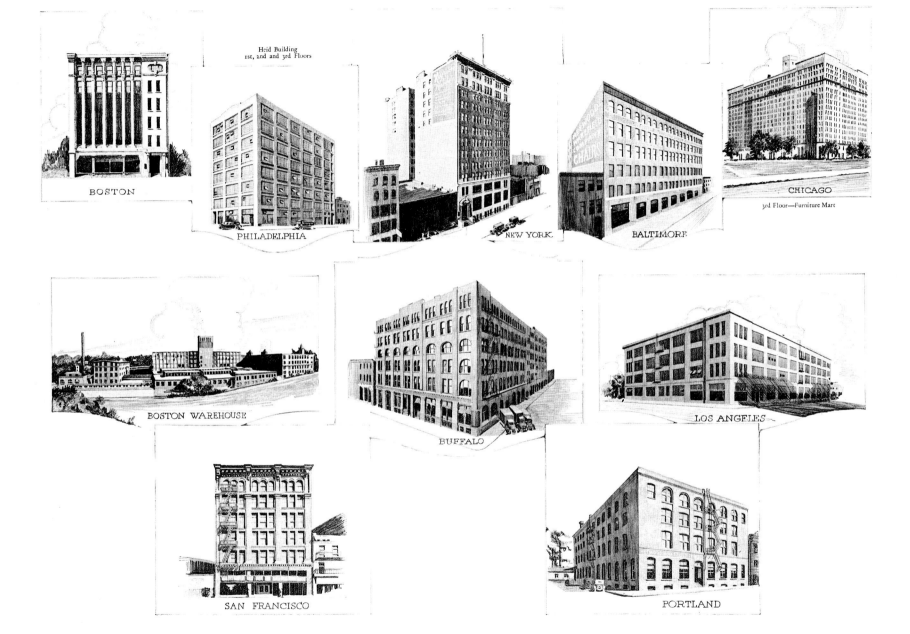

BOSTON

Heid Building
1st, 2nd and 3rd Floors

PHILADELPHIA

NEW YORK

BALTIMORE

CHICAGO

3rd Floor—Furniture Mart

BOSTON WAREHOUSE

BUFFALO

LOS ANGELES

SAN FRANCISCO

PORTLAND

Heywood-Wakefield Warehouses

Other Books From...
Schiffer Publishing